The Gospel of the Kingdom

By Philip Mauro

PANTIANOS
CLASSICS

Published by Pantianos Classics

ISBN-13: 978-1-78987-447-1

First published in 1927

Contents

Introduction

THROUGH an incident of recent occurrence I was made aware of the extent--far greater than I had imagined--to which the modern system of dispensationalism has found acceptance amongst orthodox christians; and also of the extent--correspondingly great--to which the recently published "Scofield Bible" (which is the main vehicle of the new system of doctrine referred to) has usurped the place of authority that belongs to God's Bible alone.

The incident alluded to above is what prompted the writing of this book. For it awakened in my soul a sense of responsibility to the people of God to give them, in concise form, the results of the close examination I have been led to make of this novel system of doctrine (dispensationalism).

Let it be understood at the outset that my controversy is solely with the doctrine itself; and not at all with those who hold and teach it, or any of them. Indeed I was myself one of their number for so long a time that I can but feel a tender consideration, and a profound sympathy likewise, for all such.

Moreover, as I said in another place:

"It is obvious that, in a matter involving truth of God so vital to His entire household, personal considerations must needs be disregarded. I greatly regret having to mention by name the "Scofield Reference Bible"; but that cannot be avoided, inasmuch as it is unhappily the case that that publication has been, and is, the chief agency for promulgating the errors against which I feel called upon to protest. I deeply regret having to bring any man's name into the discussion. But we must deal with conditions as we find them. It is a matter of grief to me that a book should exist wherein the corrupt words of mortal man are printed on the same page with the holy Words of the living God; this mixture of the precious and the vile being made an article of sale, entitled a 'Bible,' and distinguished by a man's name."

It is mortifying to remember that I not only held and taught these novelties myself, but that I even enjoyed a complacent sense of superiority because thereof, and regarded with feelings of pity and contempt those who had not received the "new light" and were unacquainted with this up-to-date method of "rightly dividing the word of truth." For I fully believed what an advertising circular says in presenting "Twelve Reasons why you should use THE SCOFIELD REFERENCE BIBLE," namely, that:--

"First, the Scofield Bible outlines the Scriptures from the standpoint of DISPENSATIONAL TRUTH, and there can be no adequate understanding or rightly dividing of the Word of God except from the standpoint of dispensational truth."

What a slur is this upon the spiritual understanding of the ten thousands of men, "mighty in the Scriptures," whom God gave as teachers to His people during all the Christian centuries before "dispensational truth" (or dispensational error), was discovered! And what an affront to the thousands of men of God of our own day, workmen that need not to be ashamed, who have never accepted the newly invented system! Yet I was among those who eagerly embraced it (upon human authority solely, for there is none other) and who earnestly pressed it upon my fellow Christians. Am deeply thankful, however, that the time came (it was just ten years ago) when the inconsistencies and self-contradictions of the system itself, and above all, the impossibility of reconciling its main positions with the plain statements of the Word of God, became so glaringly evident that I could not do otherwise than renounce it.

At that time I was occupied almost exclusively with the central doctrine of the system; a very radical doctrine indeed concerning the supremely important subject of the Kingdom of God, which our Lord and His forerunner proclaimed as then "at hand," and which they both identified with the era of the Holy Spirit. [1]

According to the new dispensationalism, our Lord and John the Baptist were not proclaiming the near coming of that "Kingdom of God" which actually began shortly thereafter with the pouring out of the Holy Spirit on the day of Pentecost, and which actually was then "at hand," but were announcing a kingdom of earthly grandeur for which the carnally minded Jews and their teachers were then (and are still) vainly looking; though the earthly kingdom of Israel is not called in the Scriptures, "the Kingdom of God," and though (as is now evident enough) it was not "at hand" at all.

As I continued, however, to study this new system of teaching in its various details, I found there were more errors in it, and worse, than I had at first expected; and these, as they became evident to me, I have attempted, by occasional writings subsequently, to expose. The work, however, is not yet finished; and hence the need for the present volume. Indeed, the time is fully ripe for a thorough examination and frank exposure of this new and subtle form of modernism that has been spreading itself among those who have adopted the name "Fundamentalists." For Evangelical Christianity must purge itself of this leaven of dispensationalism ere it can display its former power and exert its former influence.

Happily, however, there is a positive and constructive side to what I am now seeking to accomplish. For the object is not merely to expose the errors of twentieth century dispensationalism, but also and mainly to set forth the great, and truly "fundamental," truths of Scripture which that system has, for those who have received it, either completely obliterated or at least greatly obscured.

Finally it is appropriate in these introductory remarks to call attention (as I shall have occasion to do once and again in the pages that follow) to the striking and immensely significant fact that the entire system of "dispensational teaching" is modernistic in the strictest sense; for it first came into existence within the memory of persons now living; and was altogether unknown even in their younger days. It is more recent than Darwinism.

Think what it means that an elaborate, ramified and comprehensive system, which embraces radical teachings concerning such vital subjects as the preaching and ministry of Jesus Christ, the character and "dispensational place" of the four Gospels, the nature and era of the Kingdom of God, the Sermon on the Mount, the Gospel of the Kingdom, and other Bible topics of first importance, a system of doctrine that contradicts what has been held and taught by every Christian expositor and every minister of Christ from the very beginning of the Christian era, should have suddenly made its appearance in the latter part of the nineteenth century, and have been accepted by many who are prominent amongst the most professedly orthodox groups of Christians! It is an amazing phenomenon indeed. For the fact is that dispensationalism is modernism. It is modernism, moreover, of a very pernicious sort, such that it must have a "Bible" of its own for the propagation of its peculiar doctrines, since they are not in the Word of God. Ample proof of this will be given in the pages that follow.

Nevertheless, what I now urge in view thereof is only:-

First, that we have in these historical facts a most cogent reason why we should, each for himself, scrutinize this modern system most carefully in the light of Scripture; and second, that the above stated fact, of the very recent origin of the system, raises the presumption that dispensationalism is not in accord with the truth of God, and is not to be accepted except upon clear and ample proof.

In concluding these introductory remarks I would point out that this modern system of "dispensational teaching" is a cause of division and controversy between those followers of Christ who ought to be, at this time of crisis, solidly united against the mighty forces of unbelief and apostasy; and further that it tends to bring the vital truth of our Lord's second coming into discredit with many, because it associates that great Bible doctrine with various speculative details for which no scriptural support can be found.

Note

1. John preached, saying, "Repent Ye; for the Kingdom of Heaven is at hand," and he announced the coming of Christ, saying, "He shall baptize you WITH THE HOLY GHOST" (Mat. 3:1,11). And Christ Himself taught a Jewish rabbi, saying, "Except a man be born of water and of THE SPIRIT, he cannot enter into the Kingdom of God" (John 3:5). Compare Paul's definition of that Kingdom: "For the Kingdom of God is not meat and drink; but righteousness, and peace, and joy, IN THE HOLY GHOST" (Rom. 14:17)

Chapter One - Twentieth Century Dispensationalism: What and Whence?

FOR some of our readers a definition of modern dispensationalism will be a necessity, and for all it will be a convenience. It has been defined as "that system of doctrine which divides the history of God's dealings with the world into periods of time, called "dispensations'." And it is an essential tenet of the system that "in each dispensation God deals with man upon a plan different from the plan of the other dispensations... Each dispensation is a thing entirely apart from the others, and, when one period succeeds another, there is a radical change of character and governing principles." (Rock or Sand, Which?, by Matthew Francis).

For example, we are told that the present era is "the dispensation of Grace," and the last preceding was "the dispensation of Law"; and therefore the teachers of the new system strain their ingenuity to show that there was no grace in the preceding "dispensation," and there is no law now; whereas in fact there is all the law of God now that there ever was, and there was abundance of the grace of God in the "former times."

In the elaboration of this crude system of error, the greatest harm has been done to the revealed truth of God concerning this present era of the Gospel. According to the prophecies of the Old Testament and the apostolical scriptures of the New as they have always been understood heretofore, this is the long looked for era of the Kingdom of God, foretold by the prophets. As Peter stated it, "All the prophets from Samuel, and those that follow after as many as have spoken, have likewise"--he had just referred to Moses--"spoken OF THESE DAYS" (Acts 3:24); and in his first Epistle he declares that the things now reported by those who preach the gospel with the Holy Ghost sent down from heaven, are the very things, including the salvation of souls, that were ministered in times past by the prophets; and that it was the very same "Spirit of Christ that was in them," Who now empowers the gospel preachers (I Pet. 1:9-12).

Likewise Paul emphatically declared that in all his preaching (which even the extremest dispensationalists acknowledge as belonging to this era of grace) he had said "none other things than those which the prophets and Moses did say should come" (Acts 26:22).

But according to "dispensational teaching" this age is "a mystery," a gap of unmeasured length intervening between the past era of the natural Israel, and a future era in which (so it is taught) that apostate nation will be reconstituted and its earthly glories will be restored and enhanced.

We are told that "this gospel era was not in the view of the prophets at all;" and this is maintained despite the plain statements of Scripture just cited above and of others to the same effect.

One of the unhappiest of the results of this violent wrenching of the "things the angels desire to look into" from the place to which the word of God assigns them, is that "the Kingdom of God" in its entirety, including "the gospel of the Kingdom" (Mat. 24:14; Acts 20:25; 28:31) has been transferred bodily from this present age, and "postponed" to an hypothetical and mythical "dispensation" yet to come. This surely is a matter of such importance as to demand the most earnest attention of every saint of God; for it does violence to both the Old Testament and the New.

A RADICAL SYSTEM OF DOCTRINE

It will be readily seen therefore, that we have here to do with a system of teaching which, whether true or false, is of the most radical sort. Hence if true, it is most astonishing that not one of the Godly and spiritual teachers of all the Christian centuries had so much as a glimpse of it; and if false, it is high time its heretical character were exposed and the whole system dealt with accordingly. And inasmuch as it contradicts what every Christian teacher, without a known exception, has held to be the indisputable truth of Scripture concerning the Gospel of God and the Kingdom of God, it clearly belongs in the category of those "divers and strange doctrines," against which we are specially warned (Heb. 13:9). For it is undeniably diverse from all that has been hitherto taught the people of God, and it is altogether "strange" to their ears. This I deem worthy of special emphasis, and hence would ask the reader to keep constantly in mind the fact of the absolute novelty of dispensationalism. For here is modernism in the strictest sense; and it is all the more to be feared and shunned because it comes to us in the guise and garb of strict orthodoxy.

WHENCE CAME THIS MODERN SYSTEM?

As regards the origin of the system: the beginnings thereof and its leading features are found in the writings of those known as "Brethren" (sometimes called "Plymouth Brethren," from the name of the English city where the movement first attracted attention) though it is but fair to state that the best known and most spiritual leaders of that movement-- as Darby, Kelly, Newberry, Chapman, Mueller and others, "whose names are in the Book of Life" "never held the "Jewish" character of the Kingdom preached by our Lord and John the Baptist, or the "Jewish" character of the Gospels (especially Matthew), or that the Sermon on the Mount is "law and not grace" and pertains to a future "Jewish" kingdom.

From what I have been able to gather by inquiry of others, (who were "in Christ before me") the new system of doctrine we are now discussing was first brought to the vicinity of New York by a very gifted and godly man, Mr. Malachi Taylor, (one of the "Brethren") who taught it with much earnestness and plausibility. That was near the beginning of the present century, either a little before or a little after. And among those who heard and were captivated by it (for truly there is some strange fascination inherent in it) was the late Dr. C. I. Scofield, who was so infatuated with it that he proceeded forthwith to bring out a new edition of the entire Bible, having for its distinctive feature that the peculiar doctrines of this new dispensationalism are woven into the very warp and woof thereof, in the form of notes, headings, subheadings and summaries. There is no doubt whatever that it is mainly to this cleverly executed work that dispensationalism owes its present vogue. For without that aid it doubtless would be clearly seen by all who give close attention to the doctrine, that it is a humanly contrived system that has been imposed upon the Bible, and not a scheme of doctrine derived from it.

A REVIVAL OF ANCIENT RABBINISM

Then as to what this modern system of teaching is, it will be a surprise to most of those who love the Lord Jesus Christ to learn that, in respect to the central and vitally important subject of the Kingdom of God, twentieth century dispensationalism is practically identical with first century rabbinism. For the cardinal doctrine of the Jewish rabbis of Christ's day was that, according to the predictions of the prophets of Israel, the purpose and result of the Messiah's mission would be the re-constituting of the Jewish nation; the re-occupation by them of the land of Palestine; the setting up again of the earthly throne of David; and the exaltation of the people of Israel to the place of supremacy in the world.

Now, seeing that a doctrine is known by its fruits, let us recall what effect this doctrine concerning the Kingdom of God had upon the orthodox Jews who so earnestly believed it in that day. And in view of what it impelled those zealous men to do, let us ask ourselves if there is not grave reason to fear its effect upon the orthodox Christians who hold and zealously teach it in our day? The effect then was that, when Christ came to His own people, proclaiming that the Kingdom of God was at hand, but making it known that that Kingdom did not correspond at all to their idea of it; when He said, "My Kingdom is not of this world," and taught that, so far from being Jewish, it was of such sort that a man must be born of the Spirit in order to enter it, then they rejected Him ("received Him not") hated Him, betrayed Him and caused Him to be put to death.

Now let it be carefully noted in this connection, that the apostle Paul, referring to what had been done to Jesus by them "that dwelt at Jerusalem and their rulers," said that the reason for their murderous act was "because they knew Him not, nor yet the voices of the prophets which are read every sabbath day", and furthermore, that "they have fulfilled them in condemning Him" (Acts 13:27). This plainly declares that it was because the Jewish teachers had misinterpreted the messages of the prophets, that they were looking for the restoration of their national greatness, instead of that which the prophets had really foretold, a spiritual Kingdom ruled by "Jesus Christ of the seed of David raised from the dead" (2 Tim. 2:18).

Have we not therefore, good reason to fear disastrous consequences from the fact that the teachers of the new dispensationalism say the Jewish rabbis were right in their interpretation of the prophecies, that the kingdom foretold by the prophets is an earthly kingdom of Jewish character, and that in fact Christ's mission at that very time was to restore again the earthly Kingdom to Israel? And why then did He not do it? The answer the dispensationalists give to this crucial question is one of the strangest features of the whole system. They say, in effect, that Christ was ready to do it, and that He would have done it, but that when He "offered" them the very thing they were ardently expecting, they (most inconsistently, it would appear) "refused the offer," whereupon it was "withdrawn" and the kingdom "postponed to a future dispensation." And when we ask for the citation of a single Scripture that mentions the alleged "offer," or its "refusal," or the alleged "withdrawal" and "postponement," not a reference is produced. And particularly, when we press the vital question, what, in case the offer had been accepted, would have become of the Cross of Calvary, and the atonement for the sin of the World, the best answer we get is that in that event, "atonement would have been made some other way." Think of it! "Some other way" than by the Cross!

Now, in view of the above facts, I do most positively insist that, whatever the conclusion one may reach after an examination of the whole subject, there is to begin with, and because of the facts just stated, a very heavy "burden of proof" resting upon those who advocate this novel and radical system of teaching. And specially I insist that, as regards the doctrine of a future restoration of national Israel, with the accompaniment of supreme earthly greatness and dominion, there are two relevant facts that should receive our most serious attention: first, that that doctrine was the very cornerstone of the creed of apostate

11

Judaism in its last stage, and the prime cause of their rejection and crucifixion of Christ; and second, that it made its first appearance among Christians near the end of the nineteenth century. These facts may not settle anything; but certainly they do impose a heavy "burden of proof" upon those who now teach that the apostate Jews were right in their interpretation of the prophets (whose "voices," the apostle declares, "they knew not," Ac. 13:27) and that christian teachers and expositors for nineteen centuries were all wrong.

SOME PRESSING QUESTIONS

Moreover, because of the springing up in our midst of this new system of doctrine, certain questions of the deepest interest to the people of God are pressing for an answer at this time. Among them are the following:

Was it any part of the work of Christ to revive and reconstitute the Jewish nation? to re-establish that people in the land that was once theirs? to revive their system of worship, etc.? Did He come to reinstate the bondwoman and her son in the family of Abraham? and to make the son of the bondwoman to be heir with the son of the free woman? Did He come to raise up again, and to make permanent, that "middle wall of partition" between Jew and Gentile, or to take it away entirely and forever? Did He come to restore the "shadows" of the old covenant, or to abolish them? These are questions of surpassing importance, and they press for settlement at the present time. We are deeply convinced that one of the most urgent matters for the Lord's servants and people in these last days is to grasp the truth that there is absolutely no salvation of any sort whatever, no hope for any human being, except "through the blood of the everlasting covenant;" that there is nothing but the abiding wrath of God for those who do not stand upon the terms of that covenant; and especially that there is absolutely "no difference" in God's sight, and in His future plans, between Jew and Gentile.

It is my purpose, in the pages that follow, to seek the scriptural answers to the above, and other questions of like import.

Chapter Two - The "Seven Dispensations" Viewed in the Light of Scripture

LET us at this point inquire what, if any, support the Bible lends to the basic idea of modern dispensationalism, namely, that God has divided all time (past and future) into seven distinct and clearly distinguishable "dispensations;" and that in each of those "dispensations" He deals with mankind upon a special plan and upon peculiar principles that differ from those of all the others.

WHAT IS A "DISPENSATION"?

And first, as regards the meaning of the word itself, it is easily to be seen, that the Biblical meaning thereof is radically different from that assigned to it by the "Scofield Bible," where it is stated that:--

"A dispensation is a period of time during which man is tested in respect to some specific revelation of the Will of God" (note to Gen. 1:28).

But in our English Version of the Scriptures the word "dispensation" is not in a single instance used to designate a period of time. Paul says, "A dispensation of the gospel is committed to me" (I Cor. 9:17); that is to say, the gospel had been entrusted to him to be dispensed by him. And the word has a like signification in other passages, all its occurrences being in the writings of the apostle Paul. Thus in Ephesians 1:10 is a reference to "the dispensation of the fulness of the times"; and the apostle is there speaking of that which God had purposed to administer or dispense in these last days. ("The fulness of the time," according to Galatians 4:4, is the era when "God sent forth His Son.").

Again in Ephesians 3:2 Paul speaks of "the dispensation of the grace of God which is given me to you-ward"; the meaning being that the ministry given him was to dispense the grace of God to the Gentiles.

And lastly, in Colossians 1:25 he refers to "the dispensation of God," that had been given him, "to fulfil the word of God"; the reference being to that which God had made him responsible to administer or dispense, in fulfilment of the word of God concerning His previously concealed purpose as to the salvation of the Gentiles. These are all the occurrences of the word.

In the English Version of the Bible, therefore, the word "dispensation" means always administration, or stewardship. Our English word "economy" comes directly from the Greek word rendered "dispensation" in the four passages above referred to. It is to be deplored that a biblical word of definite signification should have been chosen for the purpose of this new system of doctrine, and a radically different meaning assigned to it.

Then further we are told, in the words of a prominent dispensationalist, that each of these seven distinct periods of time has "a character exclusively its own," being "wholly complete and sufficient in itself," that it "is in no wise exchangeable for the others, and cannot be commingled." That is to say, each "dispensation" has its own peculiar and distinguishing characteristics, insomuch that, when one succeeds another, there is a complete and radical change in the character and principles of God's dealings with the world. So say the dispensationalists; but I find in the Scriptures no evidence to support the statement. On the contrary, I find that, in every age and era, God has accepted those who believed Him and refused those who disbelieved Him. Salvation has always been "by grace, through faith," and upon the ground of the sacrifice of Christ, the Lamb slain from the foundation of the world. Adam and Eve and Abel and Enoch and Noah and Abraham and David were one and all saved precisely as we are.

WHY SEVEN DISPENSATIONS?

And now, what warrant is there for the statement that "seven such dispensations are distinguished in the Scripture" (Scofield Bible, note to Gen. 1:28)? And how does the Scripture distinguish them?

The correct answer is that there are no "such dispensations distinguished in the Scripture." The method by which they have been arrived at is purely arbitrary, fanciful, and destitute of scriptural support; the method being to select arbitrarily some epoch, such as the Exodus, and say "here began a new dispensation." But obviously the number seven is entirely arbitrary; for it is possible, by the method described, to divide human history as recorded in the Scriptures into any desired number of "dispensations." One is at liberty to take any and every important era, as the beginning of the era of the Judges, of that of the Israelitish kingdom, that of its division into two parts, the Assyrian captivity, the return from Babylon, the destruction of Jerusalem, the preaching of Christ to the Gentiles (Acts X), and say, "Here began a new dispensation"; and he would have for his dispensational scheme all the warrant that our dispensationalists have for their's--that is to say, none at all.

And if one who searched the Scriptures for indications of dispensational divisions were to assert that there was one dispensation that extended from Abraham to David, another from David to the Babylonian captivity, and another from the Babylonian captivity to Christ, he might refer to Matthew 1:17 as lending support to his scheme; whereas for the dispensational system set forth in the Scofield Bible there is no semblance of any scriptural proof.

In laying out its scheme of the seven dispensations the Scofield Bible makes the first to be the dispensation of "Innocence," and has not much to say about that. The second we are told, is that of "Conscience," which began, our authority asserts, at the expulsion of Adam and Eve from Eden. But where is there a scrap of evidence to support the idea that this period was distinguished in any special way as regards God's dealings

14

with men, from later times? or that "conscience" figured in it any more conspicuously than in other periods? To fulfil the definitions given by the dispensationalists themselves, it is necessary that "conscience" should characterize this period exclusively; for there must be "no commingling." But the fact is that nothing is said in the Scriptures, either directly or by implication concerning the human conscience during that period of history, or concerning man's being left in those remote times to the voice of his conscience; whereas, on the other hand, much is said in the New Testament about the part conscience is to have in shaping our conduct in this gospel era, and as to the importance of having a "good conscience," a "pure conscience," a "conscience void of offense"; and about what we are to do "for conscience' sake." Thus the whole system breaks down at this initial stage; for manifestly it is impossible to confine the operations of the human conscience to the comparatively unknown period that extends from the fall of man to the flood.

Third Dispensation. This is said to embrace the period extending from the flood to the call of Abraham; and we are told that this was the dispensation of HUMAN GOVERNMENT. (Scofield Bible, note to Gen. 8:20). But upon what evidence, I ask, can it be asserted that God was in any special sense (much less in an exclusive sense) dealing with the world, during that era of time, through the medium of "human government"? The fact is that there is no mention at all of human government during that period. The only recorded event belonging to it is the building of the tower of Babel; and there is no indication of human government in connection with that event. The building of that tower was not begun, continued or ended at the command of a human governor. On the contrary, what we read is that:--

"It came to pass as they journeyed from the east, that they found a plain in the land of Shinar; and they dwelt there. And they said one to another, Go to, let us make brick...and let us build us a city, and a tower whose top may reach unto heaven; and let us make us a name" (Gen. 11:1-4).

There is no trace of human government here. But now, in this gospel era, we are specially commanded to be in subjection to human governmental authorities,--kings, rulers, and magistrates of lesser degree; and are instructed by the Scriptures that "the powers that be are ordained of God," and the civil magistrate is "the minister of God" (Rom. 13:1-4; Tit. 3:1; I Pet. 2:13, 14). Is not this quite enough to show that the scheme of seven distinct dispensations is the product of the human imagination, and destitute of biblical support? Are we not justified in concluding without going further into the subject, that the reason why the discerning Bible students of past centuries did not find the seven dispensations in the Scriptures is that they are not there?

But let us nevertheless pursue the interesting subject a little further, and give heed to what is said concerning

The Fourth Dispensation. This, according to the same authority, was the dispensation of "Promise" (S.B. note on Gen. 12:1); and it extended from the call of Abraham to the giving of the law at Mt. Sinai. This period embraced the lives of Abraham, Isaac, Jacob and Joseph. In it occurred the multiplication of their seed in Egypt, the afflictions they endured in that land, their miraculous deliverance out of it by the hand of Moses, and the giving to them of the law of God with the "statutes and judgments," which prescribed for that people the worship of God and defined their relations and duties to one another. Now I ask, wherein was that period in any special sense the "dispensation of Promise"? There were indeed promises given to the fathers of Israel during that period; but there had been promises given previously, notably that grand, all-embracing, most glorious promise recorded in Genesis 3:15, concerning the Seed of the woman; a promise that includes both "the sufferings of Christ," the coming Redeemer of the world, and also "the glories that should follow." There was also the world-embracing promise given to Noah (Gen. 9:9-17). And there were also promises in profusion in subsequent times, as for example in the era of "the law and the prophets." And it is needless to say that the New Testament Scriptures simply abound in "exceeding great and precious promises."

So there is not the slightest warrant for marking off the centuries during which the natural descendants of Jacob were being multiplied into a nation, and making that era a "dispensation" specially characterized by divine promises.

The Fifth Dispensation. This is said to be the dispensation of "Law," and it is put in the strongest possible contrast to the next succeeding "dispensation," that of "Grace." And further we are told that "This dispensation [of Law] extends from Sinai to Calvary; from the Exodus to the Cross; from Ex. 19:8, to Matt. 27:35" (S. B. notes).

Here is where some of the most serious evils of dispensationalism come clearly into view; for the aspersions which the teachers of that system cast upon the holy law of God constitute in their totality a complete and grievous misrepresentation thereof; and in certain extreme instances they assume the character of slanderous vilification. But before glancing at some of these, let it be noted that the much maligned "dispensation of law" is said to have embraced the entire lifetime of our Lord--"from Ex. 19:8 to Matt. 27:35"; for it is one of the points upon which the dispensationalists mainly insist, that the Gospels belong to the era of law, and not to that of grace; which I am bold to say is palpable and pernicious error. For as regards the termination of the era of the law, we have the word of our Lord that "The Law and the prophets were"--not until Calvary, but--"until John; since that time the kingdom of God is preached" (Lu. 16:16). And in agreement with this it is written: "For the law was given by Moses, but grace and truth came by Jesus Christ" (John 1:17).

These Scriptures declare in the plainest terms that the life and words and works of our Lord "in the days of His flesh," including the "Sermon on the Mount" (concerning which we have something special to say) belong, not in the twilight era of the law of Moses, but in the full daylight era of "grace and truth." They also make it plain that the era of "the Kingdom of God" followed immediately upon that of "the law and the prophets"; and further that the era of "the Kingdom of God," and that of "grace and truth" are one and the same. And this a matter of special importance because, as I expect to point out in some detail later on, the humanly concocted scheme of the "seven dispensations," which we are now considering, has had the effect of blotting out, for those who accept it, the illuminating truth which the Scriptures reveal concerning the Two Covenants, "the old covenant," whereof Moses was the mediator, and "the new covenant" whereof Jesus Christ is the Mediator. For the Bible clearly distinguishes those two covenants and the eras to which they respectively belong; and moreover, upon that difference depends truth of the highest value. Therefore, one object I have in view, in exposing the unfounded character of dispensationalism, is to clear the ground for the presentation of the truth concerning "THE TWO COVENANTS" (Gal. 4:24).

But apart from the palpable error of placing our Lord's life and ministry in the era of law as distinguished from that of grace, the strongest exception is to be taken to the teaching that grace was entirely absent from the era of law, even as law is said to be absent from the era of grace; this being a two-fold error. And in this connection I would particularly like to ask those who hold that view, and who place the ministry of Christ in the dispensation of law, was not His ministry a ministry of grace? and were not His words "words of grace"? I wonder that this grievous teaching does not evoke bursts of indignation from those who love the Lord and who are accustomed to go for their comfort to the Gospels.

This brings us to what the "Scofield Bible" teaches concerning the holy law which God gave at Mount Sinai to the people He had delivered out of the "iron furnace" of Egypt. And first I call attention to these extraordinary statements:

"It is exceedingly important to observe...that the Law was not imposed until it had been proposed and voluntarily accepted" (Note on Ex. 19:3). "At Sinai they (Israel) exchanged Grace for Law. They rashly accepted the Law" (Note on Gen. 12:7).

Here we have in brief the teaching (which is amplified in the writings of this new school of theology) that Israel was given an opportunity to choose between Law and Grace, that they were put under the law of God by their own choice; and further that they chose "rashly," and hence made, "not a bad choice merely, but--one that was fatal, if so be that the differences between Law and Grace are what the dispensationalists aver.

As to this I say, first of all, that it is palpable error. For no choice was presented to Israel between Law and Grace, or between Law and any alternative. On the contrary, it was an essential part of God's plan in taking them out of Egypt, which He accomplished by signs and by wonders and by a mighty hand, that He might have a people who should be the custodians of His law. Thus, Psalm 105 recites the fact that the giving of the law was in fulfilment of God's covenant with Abraham (vv. 8-10). And it goes on to recall how He delivered them out of Egypt by the hand of Moses and Aaron, led them by the pillar of cloud and fire, gave them food in the desert and water out of the rock; and all to the end "That they might observe His statutes and keep His laws" (v. 45).

It is quite plain from the account given in Exodus, and also from references to the wondrous event in many later Scriptures, that the giving of the law at Mt. Sinai was God's act alone; and also that it was an act of grace and goodness. The reason He gave them His "fiery law" was because "He loved the people." Yet the teaching of the "Scofield Bible" is that the people of Israel made a fatally bad choice in consenting to be under the law of God. The statement that "they rashly accepted the Law" implies that they acted without due consideration, and did not know what they were doing or what would be the consequences of their rash choice. And this necessarily implies that God acted unfairly toward them; that He took advantage of their ignorance concerning what it meant to be "under the law," that He thus led them into a deadly trap from which it was impossible thereafter for them or their posterity to extricate themselves.

But nothing could be farther from the truth. For the gift of law to Israel was both a distinguished honor and an unspeakable benefit. It gave them the knowledge of the true God; it gave them a way of access to Him for worship and for obtaining mercies and blessings; it gave them a sanctuary, a priesthood, acceptable sacrifices--including a sin-offering-- and promises such that, by meeting the fair and reasonable conditions, they might have been a "peculiar treasure" to God and "a kingdom of priests and an holy nation" forever (Ex. 19:4, 5). Therefore, if it be asked, "What advantage then hath the Jew," over all other nations in the world? the inspired answer is, "Much every way: Chiefly because that UNTO THEM WERE COMMITTED THE ORACLES OF GOD" (Rom. 3:1).

Most certainly the Scripture last quoted could never have been written if Israel had been put under law by their own choice, and if their choice had been a bad one; for it declares that the Jew, so far from being put at a disadvantage, enjoyed much advantage and in every respect; and that the chief of all their advantages was that unto them had been committed the oracles of God---the law and the prophets.

This subject, however, is too large and too important to receive proper notice at this stage of our inquiry. So we reserve it for further consideration later on.

The Sixth Dispensation. The sixth place in the dispensational scheme we are examining is assigned to Grace. And well may we rejoice that "the grace of God that bringeth salvation hath appeared" (Tit. 2:11). But it is quite another thing to say that God's Grace characterizes this era exclusively; that Law and Grace cannot be commingled; and that "They are as far asunder as Mount Sinai and the place called Calvary, and can no more mingle than the iron and clay of Nebuchadnezzar's dream-statue."

The truth in this regard is that there was grace during the era of the Law, and that there is law during this era of the Gospel; that the New Covenant is the completion of the Old; and that the Gospel of God finishes the work that was begun by the Law of God. It would seem from the language our Lord used in Matthew 5:17 that He had this very error in view; for His words were "Think not that I am come to destroy the law or the prophets: I am not come to destroy, but to fulfil." And likewise Paul, in the question he asks and answers concerning the Gospel: "Do we then make void the law through faith? God forbid: yea, we establish the law."

Further consideration of this subject likewise must be deferred to a later chapter; so we will only add that the great difference between the past era and the present in respect to the law is that then the law of God was engraved upon tables of stone, whereas now it is written upon the hearts of His redeemed people (2 Cor. 3:3; Heb. 8:10).

The Seventh Dispensation. This, according to the most commonly held dispensational scheme, will be the Millennium; though some give a dispensational place to a supposed "great tribulation," or "time of Jacob's trouble," which they hold to be yet to come. But inasmuch as our present concern is not with any conjectural dispensations yet in the future, we shall pass this part of the general subject by without comment.

Chapter Three - The Law and the Gospel

THE Bible distinguishes--not seven dispensations, each having a character exclusively its own, but two great eras of God's dealings with mankind; the first of which was preparatory to the second, and the second of which is the completion of the first. Their scriptural designations are:

First: The Old Covenant; or the Law and the Prophets; or simply, the Law. Second: The New Covenant; or the Kingdom of God; or simply, the Gospel.

This division is not man-made, artificial, conjectural; for it comes to us plainly marked in the structure of the Bible itself, which is composed of two grand divisions, the Old Testament, and the New Testament. (And it should be noted that the word "Testament" is one of the renderings of a Greek word that is sometimes, as in Hebrews 8:6-10, and should be always, translated "Covenant").

Furthermore those two grand divisions of the Bible are clearly marked and separated, the one from the other, by the long stretch of time that intervened between them, there being a period of four hundred years between the last Book of the Old Testament and the first events (Luke I) recorded in the New. GOD HAS SPOKEN: TO THE FATHERS---TO US.

This scriptural division of God's dealings with men into two great eras is referred to in a number of passages. I have already cited Luke 16:16, "The law and the prophets were until John: since that time the Kingdom of God is preached," and John 1:17, "For the law was given by Moses, but grace and truth came by Jesus Christ." Another passage that clearly distinguishes them and also sheds light upon the whole subject is Hebrews 1:1, 2, "God, who at sundry times and in divers manners spoke in time past unto the fathers by the prophets, hath in these last days spoken unto us by His Son."

By this passage we learn that God has spoken in two different eras: (1) "in time past," and (2) "in these last days." Here we have something certain, and therefore we can safely build upon it. How valuable is the information that these days of the Gospel of Christ are "the last days"! But the dispensationalists must explain away the meaning of these words because, for one reason, their scheme provides for at least one dispensation after the termination of the Gospel era. There are, however, other passages that confirm and settle the meaning of this one. Thus Peter, speaking of the pouring out of the Holy Spirit on the day of Pentecost, said: "This is that which was spoken by the prophet Joel: And it shall come to pass in the last days saith God, I will pour out of my Spirit upon all flesh" (Acts 2:16, 17); which plainly locates the day of Pentecost in the era which God's Bible calls "the last days."

Likewise the same apostle writes concerning Jesus Christ as the Lamb of God, without blemish and without spot, saying: "Who verily was foreordained before the foundation of the world, but was manifest in these last times for you." (I Pet. 1:19, 20). And the apostle John says with characteristic brevity and emphasis: "Little children, it is the last time" (I John 2-18).

Then we have the words of Paul who, referring to the things that befell the Israelites in the wilderness, said: "Now all these things happened unto them for ensamples; and they are written for our admonition upon whom the ends of the world (lit, the ends of the ages) are come" (I Cor. 10:11). And again it is written concerning the first coming of Christ that "now once in the end of the world hath He appeared to put away sin by the sacrifice of Himself" (Heb. 9:26). It is worthy of special note that this last passage contains the adverb of time, "now," emphasizing the fact that the period of our Lord's coming and of His sacrifice belongs to "the end of the ages." We recall that the "Scofield Bible" places it in the era of the law, and does so for the purpose of separating His words (and particularly His Sermon on the Mount) from us, God's children, and allocating them to an imaginary Jewish Kingdom of a supposed future dispensation. How satisfying to the heart, and how fatal to this modernistic and pernicious error are the words of Hebrews 1:1, 2, quoted above, which plainly declare that God "hath in these last days spoken UNTO US by His Son"!

THE LAW OF MOSES AN UNSPEAKABLE BLESSING TO ISRAEL

And now as regards the character of God's dealings with those who were under the Law and the character of the Law itself, it is difficult indeed to account for and more difficult to speak calmly of, the terms of disparagement and strong repugnance in which the leaders of the dispensationalists express themselves when speaking of the Law of God. Of our Lord it was prophesied that He should "magnify the law and make it honorable," but the aim of many of His ministers in these days seems to be to belittle the law and make it detestable. Take a few specimens from the writings of prominent dispensationalists: "The Law is a ministry of condemnation, death, and the divine curse." So says the Scofield Bible (notes to Gal. 3:24). But does God's Bible speak that way? We shall see. And another leading dispensationalist declares that, "The law was the instrument of condemnation, and only that." In fact, the leaders among the dispensationalists seem to take a delight---not as did the Psalmists, "in the Law of the Lord" (Ps. 1:2), but---in inveighing in terms of strongest reprobation against it. In support of this view of the Law, reference is commonly made to certain passages in Galatians, and also to the seventh Chapter of Romans, which are misinterpreted in such a way as to cause them to render a semblance of support to that view. But before we

21

examine those passages let us get the testimony of Scripture, which is clear and unequivocal, as to what the character of the Law actually is. We have already cited the testimony of Moses that the Law delivered at Sinai was God's love-gift to the people (Deut. 33:3). It is further stated in that inspired record of "the blessing wherewith Moses the man of God blessed the children of Israel before his death," that "they sat down at Thy feet; every one shall receive of Thy words" (v. 3). And he goes on to say: "Moses commanded us a law," and that that law is "the inheritance of Jacob" (v. 4).

A number of passages earlier in the Books of Moses reveal that the law was given as a means of life. Thus, in Deuteronomy 4:1, Moses exhorts Israel to hearken to the statutes and judgments which (he says) "I teach you for to do them, that ye may live." (And to the same effect see Leviticus 18:5.) And concerning God's law he says: "For this is your wisdom and your understanding in the sight of the nations, which shall hear these statutes and say, Surely this great nation is a wise and understanding people... For what nation is so great, that hath statutes and judgments so righteous as all this law" (Deut. 4:6-8). Thus the Law of God was given the people of Israel to be their life; and it constituted their wisdom, their understanding, and their greatness in the sight of all other nations. And a little farther on Moses says: "And the Lord commanded us to do all these statutes, to fear the Lord our God, for our good always, that He might preserve us alive... And it shall be our righteousness, if we observe to do all these commandments." (Deut. 6:24, 25). And he tells them that it was because the Lord loved them that He had redeemed them out of Egypt; and that "He is the faithful God, which keepeth covenant and mercy with them that love Him and keep His commandments" (Deut. 6:8, 9). Thus, they were to love Him, because He first loved them; and they were to manifest their love by keeping his commandments. And is it any different now? Is it not written, "We love Him, because He first loved us" (John 4:19)? And does not our Lord say to us, even as he said to them "If ye love Me, keep My commandments" (John 14:15)?

Finally, before leaving Moses, we call attention to Deuteronomy 30:11-20, where he tells the people that the commandment which was to be their life, was not hidden from them (for God had revealed it to them) nor was it far off. It was not in heaven, neither was it beyond the sea; but it had been brought very nigh to them that they might hear it and do it. "And His commandments are not grievous" now (I John 5:3); nor were they grievous then. For on that occasion Moses gave as the great commandment of the law, "to love the Lord thy God, to walk in His ways, and to keep His commandments and His statutes and His judgments" (cf. Matt. 22:37). And he repeats in verse 20 the exhortation that they would "love the Lord," and "obey His voice"; and for the reason that "He is thy life, and the length of thy days."

According to Paul, the word which Moses had said was "nigh" into them, not afar off (in heaven or across the sea) was the very same "word of faith which we preach" (Rom. 10:8-13); citing in proof thereof two O.T. passages: "Whosoever believeth in Him shall not be ashamed" (Isa. 28:16); and "Whosoever shall call upon the Name of the Lord shall be saved" (Joel 2:32).

Likewise Peter testifies that the things ministered by the prophets during the era of the Law are the same that are now proclaimed by those who preach the Gospel (I Pet. 1:12). We are not saying, of course, that it is not a far better thing to be under Grace than under Law; for truly God has "provided some better thing for us" (Heb. 11:40), but we are seeking the testimony of God's Bible as to the character of His law, which the "Scofield Bible" grievously maligns; and its testimony as to just what it meant to the Israelites to be under the law of God instead of being left to their own ways, as were the heathen all around them. And we have seen that Moses, the mediator of that Old Covenant, declared to them repeatedly that, in the possession of the law of God they were unspeakably blessed, and chiefly in that it provided a way of life for all who set their hearts to obey it. Looking a little further we note that the Book of Psalms opens with a glowing reference to the blessedness of the man whose "delight is in the law of the Lord," and who meditates in it "day and night" (Ps. 1:2). And there are other passages, not a few, which testify that the law of God was a thing in which the heart of man could (and therefore should) find delight, and find also profitable meditations continuously (Job. 23:12; Ps. 119:70, 77, 92, 174).

Now as to the effects of the law, so far from it being true that it was "the instrument of condemnation and only that," or "a ministry of condemnation, death, and the divine curse," the testimony of the Holy Spirit is that "the law of the Lord is perfect, converting the soul"; and that "the commandment of the Lord is pure, enlightening the eyes" (Ps. 19:7, 8). And the same Psalm declares as to the value of the commandments and judgments of the Lord, that they are "More to be desired than gold. Yea, than much fine gold"---more intrinsically valuable than great quantities of the richest treasures of earth---and that, so far from being distasteful and obnoxious, they are "sweeter also than honey and the droppings of honeycombs" (v. 10, marg.).

The writer of Psalm 119 adds his testimony that there are wondrous things to be seen in the law (v. 18); that it was better to him "than thousands of gold and silver" (v. 72); that he loved it beyond his power to express (v. 97); that by its precepts he got understanding, and learned thereby to hate every false way (v. 104); and that "great peace have they which love thy law; and nothing shall offend them" (v. 165).

Solomon too bears witness that "the commandment is a lamp, and the law is light" (Prov. 6:23); and that "the law of the wise is a fountain of life" (13:14). Light and life were surely there for all who sought them; and many sought and found. Solomon also records the words, "Keep My commandments and live, and my law as the apple of thine eye" (7:2).

Isaiah, in foretelling some of the glorious things that Christ (whom God designates in that passage as "My Servant") should accomplish, says that God had given Him "for a light of the Gentiles"; and that "He will magnify the law and make it honorable" (Is. 42:6, 21). Is not this a rebuke to those who traduce the law and make it despicable? Likewise during the Babylonian captivity God, in recounting the great things He had wrought for Israel and His many acts of mercy on their behalf, emphasizes the giving of the law as one of the chief of them, saying: "And I gave them my statutes and showed them my judgments, which if a man do, he shall even live in them" (Ezek. 20:11).

Also through Hosea, God, in recounting the offences of Israel, said: "I have written to him the great things of My law; but they were counted as a strange thing" (Hos. 8:12). And through the very last of the prophets of Israel, and in almost the last words of his message, God calls to them: "REMEMBER YE THE LAW OF MOSES MY SERVANT, WHICH I COMMANDED UNTO HIM IN HOREB FOR ALL ISRAEL, WITH THE STATUTES AND JUDGMENTS" (Mal. 4:4).

Is it possible in the face of these testimonies to maintain that the law was imposed" upon Israel because of their own improvident choice? that "At Sinai they exchanged Grace for Law; they rashly accepted the law"? or that "The Law is a ministry of condemnation, death, and the divine curse," an instrument of "pitiless severity"? If not, shall we allow these false and derogatory things concerning the holy, life-giving and soul-enlightening law of our God to be any longer preached and taught amongst us without earnest protest on our part?

This is a serious matter indeed; and therefore I trust that my readers may be moved to join in a solemn protest against the further publication and sale of a book that many unwary children of God accept as a "Bible," and which contains so grievous a misrepresentation "amounting to a vilification" of the holy Law of God.

WHAT THE NEW TESTAMENT SAYS CONCERNING THE LAW

But it will be asked whether God's servants under the New Covenant, the apostles of our Lord who have been taught by Grace, do not give a different character to the Law, from that ascribed to it by Old Testament writers. We have quoted the words of Christ that He came not to destroy the law and the prophets, but to fulfil them; and also Paul's word to the same effect, that the purpose of the Gospel is to "establish the Law." Further our Lord declared that "the weightier matters of the law," which the Pharisees had omitted, are "judgment, mercy, and faith" (Matt. 23:23).

The apostle Paul also, whose words are cited as authority for the teaching we are now examining, speaks clearly and forcefully to the same effect. He says that "the righteousness of God," which is now manifested apart from the law (i.e. by the gospel) was "witnessed by the law and the prophets" (Rom. 3:21). Further he declares that "the commandment" was "ordained TO LIFE"; that "the law is holy, and the commandment is holy and just and good"; and that "the law is spiritual" (Rom. 7:10, 12, 14); which testimonies carry the more weight because they are found in that very passage which is supposed to teach things derogatory to the law.

But does not Paul say that the law brought death and a curse? that those who are under the law are under a curse? and that no one can be justified by the law? The reply is that the law is indeed a two-edged sword, bringing life to those who submissively receive it and who set their heart to obey it; but bringing death and condemnation and a curse to those who despise it, or who only profess respect for it with the lips while in their hearts they continue unchanged in their own ways. But precisely the same thing is true of the Gospel. For the ministry of the gospel, like that of the law, while a ministry of "life unto life" to all who with humility receive and submissively "obey the gospel," is likewise a "savour of death unto death" to all who refuse it, or neglect it, or who profess with the mouth, but continue unchanged at heart (2 Cor. 2:16). For the word of Christ is salvation and life to all who receive it; but concerning him that receives not His words He Himself has said: "The word that 1 have spoken"---the very word that was given for his salvation---"the same shall judge him at the last day" (John 12:48). Precisely so is it with the commandment of God; for in that very passage Christ declared that "His commandment is life everlasting" (v. 50).

Indeed, the consequences threatened to "them that obey not the gospel" are represented as being even more severe than those threatened to them who refused obedience to the law (2 Thess. 1:7-10). And in Hebrews 10:28, 29 it is put this way: "If he that despised Moses' law died without mercy;---of how much sorer punishment, suppose ye, shall he be thought worthy, who hath trodden under foot the Son of God"--etc.

Returning to Paul, we note that after saying that "the commandment was ordained unto life," he immediately adds that he "found it to be unto death" (Rom. 7:10). Why so? Because Paul was a Pharisee. He had been thoroughly indoctrinated into rabbinism, one of the cardinal doctrines of which was this very teaching as to the earthly and "Jewish" character of the Kingdom which has become the cornerstone of modern dispensationalism. He had been schooled in a barren orthodoxy. He was "called a Jew," and made his "boast of the law" (Rom. 2:17, 18, 23); but he had yet to learn that "He is not a Jew"---though "called a Jew"--"who is one outwardly;...but he is a Jew who is one inwardly" (vv. 28, 29).1 Of course to such it will be found that the law was "unto death"; and precisely so with the gospel. But all who were like Ezra, of whom it is recorded that he "prepared his heart to seek the law of the Lord, and to do it" (Ezra 7:10) have found that it was indeed "ordained unto life." Paul clearly states the principle here involved when he says, "But we know that the law is good, if a man use it lawfully" (I Tim. 1:8). And the same is true of the gospel as well.

Then as regards the statement often heard in these days, that those who were under the law were under a curse, what Paul says is that "as many, as are of the works of the law are under the curse" (Gal. 3:10) which is quite another thing. For Paul is here remonstrating with those who were relying for their salvation upon the rites and ceremonies (the "works") of the law, upon circumcision, keeping of days and the like. "A man," he says, "is not justified by the works of the law, but by the faith of Jesus Christ" (Gal. 2:16). So it was under the Law precisely as now under Grace. And it should not be necessary to say that a man can no more be saved by christian rites and observances (baptism, the Lord's supper, keeping holy days etc.) than by those of Judaism. So the apostle declared in another place, saying, that "Israel, which followed after the law of righteousness, hath not attained to the law of righteousness. Wherefore?" (Was it because righteousness was unattainable by the law? Not at all; but) "Because they sought it not by faith, but as it were by the works of the law" (Rom. 11:7); and as we have seen from the word of Christ Himself, faith is one of "the weightier matters of the law"; and of course no amount of "the works of the law" will serve instead.

Continuing in Galatians, Paul asks whether they had received the Spirit "by the works of the law, or by the hearing of faith" (3:2); and whether he himself, who had ministered to them the Spirit and had wrought miracles among them, had done it "by the works of the law, or by the hearing of faith" (v. 5). And then he declares that--so far from what the dispensationalists teach as to there having been a complete change in the principles of God's dealings with men--God acts now upon precisely the same principles as of old, "Even as Abraham believed God, and it was counted to him for righteousness." And adds as a corollary: "Know ye therefore, that they which are of faith, the same are the children of Abraham" (v. 7).

This verse clearly identifies those who are to inherit the promises made "to Abraham and his seed" (v. 16), and it completely rules out the natural descendants of Abraham. The last verse confirms this; for there we read, "And if ye be Christ's then are ye Abraham's seed, and heirs according to the promise" (v. 29). And this, as most impressively shown by the "allegory" in the next chapter, makes it evident that there remain no unfulfilled promises of blessing for the natural Jews as such. To this I hope to return.

Further in chapter III of Galatians, Paul takes up the question whether the law is against the promises of God" (v. 21). According to dispensational teaching the answer would be "yes." For, as we have seen, the so-called "dispensation of promise," which embraced the lives of Abraham, Isaac, Jacob, Joseph and their descendants for several generations, terminated at Mt. Sinai where Israel "rashly accepted the law"; and thereupon a new dispensation (the law, with its ministry of condemnation, death and the curse, and with a character and ruling principles totally different) was inaugurated. Thus it is clearly the teaching of the Scofield Bible that the law is against the promises of God. But Paul rejects with indignation the idea that "the law" is in anywise contrary to "the promises of God," saying: "God forbid" (v. 21); and he goes on to show that the law had a great purpose to fulfill introducto ry to the coming of the One who was to accomplish eternal righteousness and to be the Fountain of eternal life to all the world. For he says: "Wherefore the law was our schoolmaster"; and what for? "to bring us unto Christ, that we might be justified by faith" (v. 24). And he adds: "But after that faith is come, we are no longer under a schoolmaster" (v. 25). So far, therefore, from speaking with disparagement of that divinely-given "schoolmaster," or saying that his ministry was useless and worse, he shows that it was most necessary and important. It did not vacate the previously given promises. It did not introduce a new era characterized by contradictory principles; but "It was added" (to what God had previously done) "because of transgressions, till the Seed should come to whom the promise was made" (v. 19). And a further purpose of the law, in preparation for the gospel, was "that every mouth might be stopped, and ALL THE WORLD BECOME GUILTY BEFORE GOD" (Rom. 3:19).

Following further the teaching of Galatians, we find that the law as given from Mt. Sinai on tables of stone was suited to an immature stage of God's dealings with the world (Gal. 4:1-4); and that the subsequent giving of the law into the hearts of a blood-washed people by the Holy Spirit (vv. 5-7) was the mark of the mature or adult stage of the same living person (so to speak). And from this we learn that the gospel, so far from being antagonistic to the law, sustains with respect thereto the same relation that the adult period of a man's life bears to his childhood.

And in this connection, the pertinent lesson for our present purpose is that "the works of the law" against which Paul was warning the Galatians (the observing of "days and months, and times, and years," (v. 10) and circumcision (5:2, 6), belonged to the childhood stage of God's dealings with His people. And it was for that reason that though they served useful purposes for a certain period, they were to be laid aside as outgrown things, now that "the fulness of the time was come (v. 4). As Paul said in another place: "When I was a child, I spake as a child, I understood as a child, I thought as a child; but when I became a man, 1 put away childish things" (I Cor. 13:11)--not, be it noted, because they were detestable or reprehensible, but simply because they were outgrown, and would be a hindrance to the duties of manhood.

We see therefore, that the very passages that are used now-a-days to breed feelings of aversion toward the law of God, and to make it appear as something wholly antagonistic to the gospel, teach the very contrary; namely, that the law was a stage of the divine work preliminary to that of the gospel; or in other words, that the law and the gospel are complementary stages of one and the same great work of God.

For the truth in this regard is, as has been taught all through the christian centuries, that the law was a necessary part of God's great plan of Redemption even as is the Gospel. And as an excellent specimen of what enlightened servants of Christ, men who were mighty in the Scriptures, had always taught concerning the relation of the Law to the Gospel (before dispensationalism was invented) I quote the following from Bernard's celebrated work, The Progress of Doctrine.

"A principle that is contended for and secured (by Christ's apostles in their teaching) is that the Gospel is the heir of the Law; that it inherits what the Law had prepared.

"The Law, on its national and ceremonial side, had created a vast and closely woven system of ideas. These were wrought out and exhibited by it in forms according to the flesh "an elect nation, a miraculous history, a special covenant, a worldly sanctuary, a perpetual service, an anointed priesthood, a ceremonial sanctity, a scheme of sacrifice and atonement, a purchased possession, a holy city, a throne of David, a destiny of dominion. Were these ideas to be lost? and was the language that expressed them to be dropped when the Gospel came? No! It was the heir of the Law. The Law had prepared these riches; and it now bequeathed them to a successor able to unlock and diffuse them. The Gospel claimed them all, and developed in them a value unknown before. It asserted itself as the proper and predestined continuation of the covenant made of God with the fathers, the real and only fulfilment of all that was typified and prophesied; presenting the same ideas which had been before embodied in the narrow but distinct limits of carnal forms in their spiritual, universal, and eternal character.

"The body of types according to the flesh died with Christ; and with Christ it arose again, a body of antitypes according to the Spirit. Those who were after the flesh could not recognize its identity; those who were after the Spirit realized and proclaimed it. The change was as great, the identity was as real, as in that mystery of the resurrection of the body which the same preachers showed; in which the earthly frame must lay aside the flesh and blood which cannot inherit the Kingdom of God, and must reappear; dead and raised again; another and yet the same; 'sown in weakness and raised in power, sown in dishonor and raised in glory, sown a natural body and raised a spiritual body.'"

Note

1. In passing let it be noted that, by the light of this verse, it may be seen that all the promises of God which read to Israel or to the Jews, are for the true "Israel" (Rom. 9:6; Gal. 6:16), and the real Jews. See the passage herein on "ISRAEL HATH NOT OBTAINED; BUT THE ELECTION HATH OBTAINED IT." (p. 236).

Chapter Four - The Beginning of the Gospel of Jesus Christ, The Son of God

THE words of our chapter heading are the first words of the Gospel by Mark. They are enlightening words; and indeed they are quite sufficient in themselves to answer a question that confronts us at this point: When did the Gospel era begin? It is exceedingly important that we should have the right answer to that question; and we know where to seek it.

We have seen that the Bible distinguishes two great eras, and those two eras are closely related, the one to the other, though there are marked differences between them; the first being variously designated as, "the old covenant," "the law and the prophets," or simply "the law"; and the second being variously designated as, "the new covenant," "the kingdom of God," or simply "the gospel." Our Scripture tells us we are now at the "beginning" of something; and that that something is "the gospel of Jesus Christ." Could we have a plainer answer to our question?

And the passage goes on to tell what it was that marked "the beginning of the gospel"; and further to declare that the event that marked it was something that had been foretold in the Scriptures. For we read: "As it is written in the prophets, Behold, I send my messenger before Thy face, which shall prepare Thy way before Thee. The voice of one crying in the wilderness, Prepare ye the way of the Lord, make His paths straight." The reference is to Isaiah 40:3; and the prophecy was fulfilled, as this first chapter of Mark's Gospel declares, in the preaching and ministry of John the Baptist.

This was the very "beginning," the very first event of that long expected era. "THE GOSPEL OF JESUS CHRIST, THE SON OF GOD." But John's ministry was of short duration; for the enmity of the Jews was speedily aroused, because of the contradiction between his preaching and their expectations; and he was cast into prison. And then happened another event of transcendent interest; for the public ministry of Christ Himself (whose "way" John had been sent to "prepare") forthwith began. For it is written: "Now after that John was put in prison, Jesus came into Galilee, preaching the gospel of the Kingdom of God, and saying, The time is fulfilled, and the Kingdom of God is at hand: repent ye, and believe the gospel" (vv. 14, 15).

These words make it evident that "the gospel of Jesus Christ, the Son of God," and "the gospel of the Kingdom of God" are one and the same. Moreover, the words, "The time is fulfilled" manifestly point to something of exceptional importance whereof promises had been given by the prophets. They refer, of course, to that promised era of victory over sin, that era of the bruising of the serpent's head, of the salvation of God for all men through the coming of the promised Deliverer, the era of the everlasting covenant and the sure mercies of David; in a word, they referred to the appointed time for the fulfilment of all the glorious things that God had spoken by the mouth of all His holy prophets since the world began. "The time" for the thing for which all believing hearts had looked and longed, was "fulfilled." So said Christ; and He also exhorted those who heard the announcement, to repent, and believe the gospel." Note that the proclamation that the time was fulfilled He calls "the gospel."

But, in direct contradiction to these statements (which are as plain as is possible for anyone to make) the "Scofield Bible" asserts that the dispensation of the law, with its "pitiless severity" and all the appalling characteristics of condemnation, death and the curse which that publication attributes to it, continued until the crucifixion of Christ; and it further asserts that "the Kingdom of God" (which that dispensational authority takes to mean the earthly kingdom of Jewish expectancy) was not "at hand," but was in the far distant future. Here then we have a very serious situation. For if this era of John the Baptist were not "the beginning of the gospel of Jesus Christ, the Son of God," then the plainest of plain Bible words, which have been understood for nineteen centuries in accordance with their apparent sense, have a meaning altogether different to what has always been supposed. And if the Kingdom our Lord said was then "at hand," was not at hand at all, but far away, He certainly caused those who heard Him believingly and all who have listened to His words for nearly two thousand years, to believe what was not true.

We take up first the question:

What Kingdom was it that Christ said was at hand?

In considering this question let it be noted that there was a "Kingdom of God" then at hand; for Christ's servants shortly thereafter began to preach it as a present reality (Acts 8:12; 14:22; 20:25, etc.); and moreover, the apostle Paul, in his great Gospel letter, gave a definition of it (Rom. 14:17). Are there then two different Kingdoms of God; one of which was at hand, and one afar off in the future? Is God the author of confusion? And if there were two Kingdoms of God, one then close by and the other afar off, is it conceivable that the Kingdom of God which Christ said was then "at hand" was the one that was actually in the remote future?

How is it possible, I ask, for any who undertake to explain the Scriptures to arrive at the conclusion that the "Kingdom of God" which actually was "at hand," is not the "Kingdom of God" which the Lord said to be "at hand"; or, (to state it the other way) that the "Kingdom of God" which the Lord publicly declared at hand, proved to be not at hand at all; whereas, marvelous to relate! another "Kingdom of God" whereof He made no mention, was at hand?

I have carefully examined the notes of the "Scofield Bible" in quest of the explanation of this. I find on one hand that no Scripture is cited to support the editor's view; for there is not one word in the Bible to the effect that the Kingdom announced by the Lord has been "postponed" or is "in abeyance." The Lord's own statement, from first to last, never modified, but proclaimed with ever increasing emphasis, was that the Kingdom was "at hand."

But the teaching of the Scofield Bible as to the Kingdom of God is founded nevertheless upon the baseless assumption that the prophets of Israel, in predicting the coming of the Messiah and of an era of blessing, salvation and victory for His people, were foretelling the restoration of the earthly greatness of the natural Israel. Therefore the editor of the publication, having committed himself thoroughly to this startlingly novel idea, and having lost sight of the many interpretations of those prophecies in the New Testament which show that they referred (in figurative language) to Redemption and to the Spiritual Kingdom based thereon, has attempted in his notes to make the New Testament agree with his mistaken theory.

But the attempt is an impossibility. In fact the editor himself abandons it completely after carrying it partly through the Gospel of Matthew. Anyone can see this for himself who will take a little pains to examine the matter. For we have to begin with the bold but unfounded assumption that the words "Kingdom of God" and "Kingdom of heaven" in our Lord's lips meant the earthly kingdom of Israel. Then we have the equally bold and equally unfounded assumption that the supposed "offer" of the earthly kingdom to the Jews of Christ's day was rejected by them, and that, as the result of such supposed rejection, it was withdrawn and postponed; though there is no trace whatever in the inspired records of any such offer, or rejection, or withdrawal, or postponement; and though there is no hint that God's purpose to introduce the Kingdom which He had announced (and announced without any qualification whatever) was, or could have been, defeated or postponed by the action of the Jews of Christ's day. In the "notes," the alleged rejection is located at Matthew 11:20, as appears by the following statement:

"The Kingdom of heaven announced as 'at hand' by John the Baptist, by the King Himself, and by the twelve, and attested by mighty works, has been morally rejected."

Then the Lord's words recorded in Matthew 11:28, 29, are called by the editor, "The new message of Jesus--not the kingdom but rest and service"; and this, we are told, is "the pivotal point in the ministry of Jesus,"--that is to say the point at which He abandoned His message about the Kingdom's being at hand, and began to substitute a message of entirely different character.

I earnestly protest that these statements are wholly erroneous, and confidently maintain that the Lord had but one message, which was the gospel of God, and that the Kingdom which He preached while on earth and introduced when He sent the Holy Ghost from heaven, is the very "rest and service" which He offered and still offers to all the weary and heavy laden ones. [1]

Following this is a note (on Mat. 12:46) which asserts that our Lord, "rejected by Israel," now intimates the formation of the "new family of faith." But the fact is that the "new family"--composed of the children of His Father in heaven--had been previously addressed at length and in the most precise terms as to their relationship with God, in the Sermon on

32

the Mount. But inasmuch as it would upset the editor's theory completely to find any hint of the "new family" in that part of Matthew, he firmly closes his eyes to the conspicuous presentation of it in those chapters, and locates the first "intimation" of it in chapter 12. For it is as plain to any babe in Christ as the sun in the sky at noonday, that in the Sermon on the Mount God, the "Father in heaven," is speaking to His own "children" on earth, by the lips of His own Son. But that fact, so vital to all the household of God, would, if acknowledged, completely destroy the editor's theory, so he ignores and even contradicts it.

In order to obtain an appearance of support to his views, the editor states in a note on the Lord's interview with the woman of Syrophenicia, (Mat. 1:2 that "For the first time the rejected Son of David ministers to a Gentile." This is necessary to the theory we are examining; for if Christ should be found ministering to a Gentile prior to Matthew 11, that action on His part would destroy the "Jewish" and "legal" character which the editor imputes to that part of the Lord's ministry; and would demolish the theory completely. How is it possible then that the editor and associate editors and all who have been helping to correct the errors of his edition for more than a score of years, have been blinded to the fact that the Lord healed the centurion's servant, as recorded in Matthew 8:5-10, and in connection therewith used those remarkable words, "Verily, I say unto you, I have not found so great faith no not in Israel"? And how can we account for the failure on the part of all those learned men to observe the record in Matthew 4:24 that the fame of Jesus went throughout all Syria, and they brought to Him all sick people, and He healed them? And for their failure to observe also that, even before the Lord began to preach publicly in Galilee, He ministered and revealed Himself as "Christ" to the woman of Samaria, and that many of the Samaritans believed on Him? (John 4).2

These are but a few of many instances which show that the advocates of the postponement theory are mysteriously blinded to the plainest facts when those facts are in conflict with that theory; while on the other hand they claim the ability to "see" things in the text of Scripture which support their theory, although others are utterly unable to find a trace of them. But, without dwelling upon this, I would ask particular attention to the fact that, even according to the kind of proof by which our friends seek to maintain their theory, the facts concerning the centurion's servant and the Lord's personal ministry of salvation (the "living water") to the Samaritans, refute that theory completely.

Pursuing the notes of the aforesaid "Reference Bible" we come to the very important chapter 16 of Matthew's Gospel, where the "church" is first mentioned by name; and there, as a comment on verse 20, in which the Lord charged His disciples "that they should tell no man that He Jesus was the Christ" (Gr.), is the following note:

"The disciples had been proclaiming Jesus as the Christ, i.e. the covenanted King of a kingdom covenanted to the Jews and 'at hand.' The church on the contrary must be built on the testimony to Him as crucified, risen from the dead, ascended and made Head over all things to the church (Eph. 1:20-23). The former testimony was ended; the new testimony was not yet ready etc." (italics are mine).

I ask special attention to these statements, for they are of capital importance; and they embody errors of a very serious character; though happily the errors are clearly to be seen in the light of the Scripture.

1. To begin with the disciples had not been "proclaiming Jesus as the Christ," and the text to which this grievously misleading note is appended makes that fact startlingly clear. Indeed the note completely contradicts and falsifies the text, as anyone with but slight attention can see plainly. For the whole point of the Lord's words at Caesarea Philippi depends upon the fact that the disciples at last had become aware, through the revelation of God the Father, that He, Jesus, was the Christ. If they had been proclaiming Him, or if He had been proclaiming Himself in their hearing, as "the Christ the covenanted King," and had been offering to the Jews the Kingdom they were expecting, what point would there have been to His question, "But whom say ye that I am?" or to His words to Simon (when the latter made the great confession "Thou art the Christ, the Son of the living God"), that "flesh and blood" had not revealed this to him, but "My Father Who is in heaven"? Plainly it is impossible that He should have uttered those words if the statements of Dr. Scofield's note were true.

Let it not be forgotten that, according to the theory we are examining, the Lord had been preached all over the land as the Christ of God, come to set up the earthly throne of David. Yet His own question "Whom do men say that I, the Son of man am?" and the reply of the apostles, show plainly that He was practically unknown. For if He had announced Himself as Christ the King, and had been so proclaimed by His apostles, He could not have asked that question. Nor could they in that case, have said: "Some say Thou art John the Baptist, some Elias, and others Jeremias, or one of the prophets." And furthermore, if He had been publicly proclaimed as "Christ the King" He could not have charged them to tell no man that He was the Christ.

There is no ground whatever for such a misstatement; for the plain facts are that the Lord had never proclaimed Himself as Christ the King. His way had always been to let His works speak for Him (Mat. 11:4, 5; John 5:36; 10:25, etc.). The name by which He almost invariably called

Himself was "The Son of man," a name which connects Him with Gentiles as much as with Jews.

When the Lord crossed the sea with the disciples after feeding the five thousand, and stilled the wind and waves by His Word, they wondered what manner of man He was; and it is recorded in Mark 6:52, that "they considered not the miracle of the loaves; for their heart was hardened"; (literally the verse reads "they understood not by the loaves"); or in other words the great truth of His Messiahship was not yet apprehended by them. Still later, after feeding the four thousand, He had occasion again to rebuke them, saying: "Perceive ye not yet, neither understand? Have ye your heart yet hardened? Having eyes see ye not, and ears hear ye not?" And He concludes the long list of reproachful questions with the pointed one: "How is it that ye do not understand?" (Mk. 8:14:21).

From first to last then it is evident that He could not permit Himself to be proclaimed as Christ the King, until He had endured the appointed "sufferings of Christ." For whatever the "throne" which was promised to Him, whether heavenly or earthly, the only pathway to it lay through the predicted sufferings and death that awaited Him. The concurrent testimony of all the Scriptures is that the prophecies concerning David's promised Son were to be fulfilled only in resurrection. (See for example Acts 2:29-32; and 13:22-24 and 32-34). His "Father's business" upon which He had come was not at all in connection with the earthly expectations of Israel, but was for the Redemption of the whole world, and the introduction of a spiritual Kingdom composed of redeemed sinners out of every nation under heaven.

2. Consider now the following statement of the above quoted note: "The former testimony was ended, the new testimony was not yet ready." I have shown that what the editor takes to be "the former testimony," namely the testimony of Christ as King Who had come to set up the earthly kingdom, which testimony he says was "ended," had not been begun up to that time; for the apostles themselves had just apprehended that He was the Christ. It is also clear that, in the Divine program (which of course was perfectly carried out) the Lord Jesus was not to be preached as "the Christ" until He was risen from the dead and enthroned in heaven. This passage therefore is quite sufficient in itself to settle the whole question as to what sort of a "Kingdom" the Lord and His forerunner had announced. The "Christ" or "Messiah" was, according to Psalm 2, the promised King of Israel. If therefore the Lord forbade His disciples to announce Him as "the Christ," He in effect forbade them to announce Him as the King of Israel. The Scripture will be searched in vain for any occasion when they proclaimed Him as either Christ or King before He rose from the dead. In fact, before Pentecost they did not

preach the Lord Jesus--the Person--at all, but only announced the nearness of the Kingdom.

But regardless of what was meant by "the Kingdom of heaven" and "Kingdom of God," the fact is that, instead of the preaching of the Kingdom being "ended" at this point, as the theory demands and as the Scofield Bible dogmatically asserts, the very same proclamation continued right on to the end of the Lord's earthly ministry, not only with undiminished energy, but even with increased diligence. For, on His last journey to Jerusalem, during which He told His disciples again and again that He was about to be betrayed to the chief priests and scribes, and be crucified, and would rise again from the dead the third day, He appointed "other seventy," in addition to the original twelve, and set them forth to proclaim the Kingdom of God as at hand. (See for example Luke 18:31-34, and notice that subject of the Lord's discourse is the Kingdom of God. Ch. 16:16; 17:20; 18:16-30).

The appointment of those "other seventy also" is recorded in Luke 10:1-9, the sending forth of the twelve being mentioned in chapter 9, before the Transfiguration.

The sending of the seventy, with identically the same instructions and with identically the same announcement previously given to the twelve, indicates that the time was getting so short for the preliminary proclamation of the Kingdom (for the Passover at which the Lord was to be slain was but a few weeks off, they being then on the way to Jerusalem), that many additional messengers were needed to cover the ground. It shows also that the announcement of the Kingdom of God as "at hand" went side by side with the Lord's repeated explanation to His own disciples of what was to befall Him at Jerusalem; and this is proof that the Kingdom He had proclaimed awaited only His approaching death, resurrection, ascension, and enthronement in heaven as "King of Glory," in fulfilment of Psalms 2, 24, and 110. When He ascended "the throne of the Majesty in the heavens", (Heb. 8:1), then the "Kingdom of the heavens" began.

Those who hold the postponement theory realize that the announcement of Christ's sufferings and death could not possibly be coupled with that of an earthly kingdom. Hence our friends have been sorely troubled by John the Baptist's proclamation of Jesus as the Lamb of God Which taketh away the sin of the world; since they are utterly unable to explain that proclamation consistently with their theory. For that theory demands that when Christ began to tell the disciples of His approaching death He should cease to proclaim the Kingdom. If, however, His death and resurrection were necessary to the introduction of the Kingdom He had been announcing, then we should expect to find His references thereto accompanied by an even more intense preaching of the Kingdom; and that is precisely what we do find.

The instructions given to the seventy were that they should heal the sick, and preach, saying: "The Kingdom of God is come nigh unto you" (Lu. 10:9); and it should be observed that the words "is come nigh," are precisely the same in the original as the words "is at hand." So the announcement of these seventy was identical with that of the Lord Himself as recorded in Mark 1:15. And not only so: but there was an added emphasis to the announcement as thus commanded by the Lord at the very end of His ministry; for He instructed the seventy that in any city which received them not they were to go out into the streets and say: "Even the very dust of your city, which cleaveth on us, we do wipe off against you; notwithstanding be ye sure of this that the Kingdom of God is come nigh unto you" (Lu. 10:9-11).

According to the postponement theory, when the kingdom proclaimed by the Lord was rejected by the Jews, it was forthwith, and for that reason, "withdrawn" and "postponed." But, according to the Lord's own word, the messengers were to say to any cities which rejected the message, "Notwithstanding (your rejection) be ye sure of this, that the Kingdom of God is come nigh unto you." So this Scripture demolishes the theory completely.

We see then that, according to Scripture, the Lord proclaimed the Kingdom of God as "at hand" from the very beginning to the very end of His public ministry; and that, so far from abandoning the proclamation, He gave it a wider publicity toward the end. The notes of the "Scofield Bible" flatly contradict this clear record, and say that the testimony of the kingdom was ended about the time of the beheading of John the Baptist. And what is most remarkable is the fact that long after the time when, according to the "Scofield Bible," the announcement of the kingdom ceased, the Lord's messengers were, by His special command, making that very announcement everywhere with the added words "Be ye sure of this." We see then that the rejection of the message by the Jews was not to change the declared purpose of God; and how could anyone have supposed for a moment that it would? Indeed, the hatred and opposition of the Jews did but serve to accomplish the eternal purpose of God; and their attention was called to that fact by the apostle Peter, who, after accusing them of having "killed the Prince of Life," went on to say: "But those things, which God before had showed by the mouth of all His prophets, that Christ should suffer, He hath so fulfilled" (Acts 3:13-18).

Here again is a Scripture which tells plainly what was the great topic of all the prophets of God; and which also tells plainly that it was not the restoration of the Jewish nation, but the sufferings of Christ and the eternal and spiritual kingdom, "the Kingdom which cannot be shaken," that was to be founded thereon.

Notes

1. Some of the errors made in the attempt to sustain the postponement theory are almost unbelievable. Thus in an article by Dr. Scofield appearing in "Our Hope" for April, 1920, it is said that "the time speedily came when it was clear that the true King was rejected." That time he locates at the chapter we have just been considering, Matthew XI, where the Lord upbraids the cities in which His mightiest works were done. "From that moment," says Dr. S., "the message is changed; it is no longer 'the Kingdom of heaven is at hand.'" The postponement theory demands that it should be so; and therefore Dr. S. unhesitatingly affirms that it is so. But it is recorded that, as late as when the Lord was on His way to Jerusalem to die there, He sent forth--not twelve as at first, but--seventy to proclaim "the Kingdom of god is come nigh unto you" (Luke 10:9). And He instructed His disciples, in case they were rejected, to say--not that the Kingdom was withdrawn and postponed, but to say--"Notwithstanding be ye sure of this, that the Kingdom of God is come nigh unto you" (v. 11). Thus we see that just where the editor of the "Scofield Bible" says the announcement of the Kingdom ceased entirely, the Lord commanded that it be proclaimed with increasing emphasis and with greater positiveness. Extended comments on this passage will be found in the following pages.

2. The Samaritan were more despised than the Gentiles, and the Jews held themselves more aloof from the former than from the latter. For while they had many dealings with Gentiles and even accepted them as proselytes, they had "no dealings with the Samaritans" (John 4:9).

Chapter Five - The Kingdom of God: Has It Been Postponed?

INCREASINGLY conviction presses upon me that "the word of THE KINGDOM" is God's special message for these--the last days of our era--even as it was His special message for the first days thereof. We recall that when, at the beginning of our era, the Sower went forth to sow, what He sowed in His field was "the word of THE KINGDOM"; and moreover, we have His promise for it that "the end shall come" when "this gospel of THE KINGDOM" shall have been preached "for a witness to all nations." Then will "the harvest" from His sowing be gathered (Mat. 24:14; Rev. 14:15).

Therefore my conviction is that, in preaching "the good news of God concerning His Son, Jesus Christ our Lord, who was made of the seed of David" (Rom. 1:1-3), prominence should be given to the revealed truth of

Scripture concerning "the Kingdom of His dear Son" (Col. 1:13). In so doing we would be following the example of the apostles, notably that of Peter on the day of Pentecost (Acts 2:33-36). For that truth is what gave the gospel its note of authority and its unique "power" at the beginning (Rom. 1:16). It was the exaltation of Jesus, and His enthronement on high as "both Lord and Christ," that was preached by the apostles "with the Holy Ghost sent down from heaven" (Acts 2:36; 1 Pet. 1:12).

Likewise in the gospel as preached by Paul, emphasis was placed upon the fact that Jesus Christ was "of the seed of David" (the royal line) ; and that in Him are fulfilled all the prophecies and promises concerning the glorious reign of Messiah and "the sure mercies of David" (Rom. 1:3; Acts 13:34; 2 Tim. 2:8). Paul preached the Kingdom of God and of Christ as a then present reality, into which every believer of the gospel was instantly translated; having been first delivered by the mighty power of God out of the kingdom of sin and darkness (Col. 1:12, 13).

Never was there from the lips or pen of that apostle a hint or suggestion to the effect that the reign of Jesus Christ, which God had promised afore by His prophets in the Holy Scriptures, had been postponed to another era. Indeed, one cannot attentively study the elements of the gospel as preached and taught by "the apostle of the Gentiles" (except under the blinding influence of some doctrine of men) without perceiving that, apart from the word of the Kingdom there is no gospel and no salvation for perishing men. And let it not be forgotten in this connection, that it is through this same apostle, and with reference to this self same heresy of one gospel for Jews and a different gospel for Gentiles, that the curse of God is decreed upon those--be they apostles of Christ or angels from heaven--who preach any other gospel. For there is but one gospel" for all the world, and for all the ages of time; and whether it were Paul or one of the twelve, they all preached the same gospel of the Kingdom (I Cor. 15:11; Acts 20:24, 25).

If then (as often is mournfully admitted today) the gospel is lacking in power, it would be appropriate to ask, "Is there not a cause?" (I Sam. 17:29). Certainly there is a cause; and the apostle of the Gentiles points us to it when he says: "For the Kingdom of God is not in word, but in power" (I Cor. 4:20).

AS IT WAS IN THE BEGINNING

It is beyond dispute that Christ Himself and His immediate disciples preached a Kingdom. And not only so, but the word, "Kingdom," conveyed to those who heard the preaching, the very essence of the "good news which our Lord in person announced publicly, and which He exhorted and commanded His hearers to "believe" (Mk. 1:14, 15). And most important is it to observe that He coupled with His announcement the plain statement that "the time" for the long expected Kingdom of God, was then "fulfilled."

Furthermore, our Lord's earliest teaching (given while John was yet baptizing in Jordan) had for its theme the Kingdom of God, and the one and only way of entering into it--by the new birth of water and the Spirit (John 3:3-16). This best known passage in the Bible links the Kingdom of God directly with the death of Christ upon the cross, whereby God's great love for the perishing world was to be revealed, and the ground of the salvation of men was eternally established. The passage shows clearly moreover, what the term, "Kingdom of God," meant in the days of John the Baptist (vv. 23, 24). How then can any one, viewing the subject of the Kingdom in the light of this great passage, suppose for a moment (except he be under the spell of a strong delusion) that our Lord and His forerunner were at that very time offering to the Jews, and by the preaching of the Kingdom of God, a kingdom of earthly pomp and grandeur, such as their false teachers--those "blind leaders of the blind"-- had taught them to expect?

Our Lord's subject after His resurrection was precisely the same. For He remained on earth forty days, appearing frequently to His disciples, and "speaking of the things pertaining to the Kingdom of God" (Acts 1:3).

A little later, when the word was carried into Samaria by Philip (fulfilling Christ's command, recorded in Acts 1:8), what he preached was "the things concerning the Kingdom of God" (Acts 8:12). And still later, when Paul carried into Europe the message that "turned the world upside down" (Acts 17:6, 7), he came to Corinth, and spake in the synagogue, "disputing and persuading the things concerning the Kingdom of God" (Acts 19:8). For of course, there was strong opposition from the Jews to Paul's proclamation of a spiritual Kingdom, embracing all believers, and ruled by a "King invisible" (I Tim. 1:17), seeing they had received as unquestioned truth the false rabbinical teaching of an earthly kingdom exclusively Jewish. But how astounding, that the same ruinous doctrine has now, in these last days, found wide acceptance among orthodox Christian teachers!

It will not be necessary to follow in detail the record of Paul's journeyings with the gospel. It is enough to point out that to the very end of his days he continued "preaching the Kingdom of God" (Acts 28:31).

HOW THE WORD OF THE KINGDOM WAS SET ASIDE

I have already pointed out, but it is needful to keep the fact in mind, that in the latter part of the nineteenth century an extraordinary change took place in the teaching of certain groups of orthodox Christians. It was a radical change. Indeed, "revolutionary" is not too strong a term to apply to it; for the literature of the Christian centuries will be searched in vain for a trace of the new doctrine, which then suddenly sprang up, and soon spread far and wide. That new doctrine was a system of "dispensational" teaching, characterized chiefly by a wholesale and indiscriminate futurism. Every promise and prophecy was relegated to the future that could by any possibility be dealt with in that way; and thus the era of grace and the gospel of grace were stripped of what properly belonged to them--specially the blessed and glorious truth of the Kingdom--the gospel of God was robbed of its power, and grievous damage was done to the people of God, and indeed to all men.

What is central in this novel system of "dispensationalism" is the doctrine, theretofore unheard of, that Christ and His forerunner, when they announced that the Kingdom of God was at hand, were thereby "offering" to the Jews the earthly kingdom of their grossly carnal expectations; that (astonishing to relate) the Jews refused what they most eagerly looked for, when it was thus proffered to them; and that thereupon God withdrew the offer and "postponed" the Kingdom to another "dispensation."

The Scriptures, however, contain not a word about this offer of an earthly, Jewish kingdom, or about the refusal thereof by that generation of Jews, or about its postponement to another dispensation. Nevertheless it is claimed on behalf of this novel doctrine that it is newly discovered truth, which has been brought to light by a recently invented process of "rightly dividing the word of truth."

Thus the matter stands at the present time; and while there have been of late some encouraging indications of a healthy reaction against this mischievous postponement heresy, there is yet need of earnest, prayerful effort, on the part of all who have been enlightened as to its real character and consequences, to the end that the sadly neglected and truly vital truth of the Kingdom of God may be restored to its rightful and central position in "the gospel of God concerning His Son."

And whatever the reader's convictions as to the doctrine that the Kingdom which Christ announced as at hand has been postponed, the truth involved is so vital, and the postponement doctrine is so startlingly novel, that it is the duty of all who belong to Christ to examine, and to re-examine, the whole subject with the utmost care; and to give an attentive hearing to anyone who asks their consideration of evidence from the word of God. That is what I am now asking. And as a reason why a fair hearing should be given me, I solemnly declare my deep conviction that so closely is the Kingdom of God identified with the Salvation of God, that

41

if this be not the era of the former, then it is not the era of the latter. Proof of this I present in this chapter.

For example, in Isaiah 49:5-9 is a glorious prophecy concerning Christ, God's "Servant," His "Holy One," Who was to raise up the tribes of Jacob and restore the preserved of Israel; and Who was also to be for "a light to the Gentiles, that He might be "My salvation unto the end of the earth." Now as to the time when this should be, read in verse 8 the familiar words: "Thus saith the Lord, In an acceptable time have I heard thee, and in. a day of salvation have I helped thee."

If therefore "to raise up the tribes of Jacob and to restore the preserved of Israel" means the restitution of the earthly nation to its place of eminence in the world, as the dispensationalists hold and teach, then certainly the fulfilment of this prophecy must be yet in the future. But the apostle Paul refutes that idea completely when, writing to a Gentile church, he says and with the strong emphasis of repetition: "Behold, NOW is the accepted time; behold, NOW is the day of salvation" (2 Cor. 6:2). Manifestly, if now is the accepted time, and now is the day of salvation, it is impossible that there should be any other "accepted time," or any other "day of salvation"; and doubly impossible that what God promises in this particular prophecy to be for "Israel" and for "the tribes of Jacob" could be accomplished in a different and later "dispensation."

It is appropriate here to point out that one of the glaring errors of "dispensational teaching" is the failure to recognize what the New Testament plainly reveals, namely that names which God temporarily gave to the shadowy and typical things of the Old Covenant, belong properly and eternally to the corresponding realities of the New Covenant. Thus we are given the proper meaning of "Jew" (Rom. 2:28, 29;) "Israel" (Rom. 9:6; Gal. 6:16) ; "Jerusalem" (Gal. 4:26); "Seed of Abraham" (Gal. 3:29); "Sion" (I Pet. 2:6; Heb. 12:22; Rom. 9:33). Likewise it is made known that according to the new covenant meaning, "the tribes of Jacob" are those who are Jews inwardly, that is to say, the entire household of faith (James 1:1; Acts 26:7).

And then that the gospel of the kingdom and the gospel of salvation are one and the same thing;--seeing that the responsibility of a king is to save his people, this is clearly indicated by the word of the Lord to Israel through Hosea: "O Israel, thou hast destroyed thyself, but in Me is thy help. I will be thy King; where is any other that may save thee?" (Hos. 13:9). So here is a distinct promise to Israel that the Lord would come as King to save; and this is but one of many passages which associate salvation with the Kingdom of God. Then in verse 14 the nature of the salvation that is promised here through Christ the King of Israel is unmistakably indicated by the familiar words: "I will ransom them from the power of the grave; I will redeem them from death: O death, I will be thy plagues; O grave, I will be thy destruction."

The meaning and the significance of this are plain enough to the unsophisticated; but let it be noted additionally that, in the passage where this is quoted in the N.T., the great resurrection chapter (I Cor. 15:54, 55) Paul declares in the immediate context the vital truth that "flesh and blood CANNOT inherit the Kingdom of God" (v. 50). This is proof positive and conclusive, first, that the Kingdom of God is the inheritance of those who are saved by the gospel (vv. 1-4); and second, that the Kingdom of God is not the restoration of the earthly Jewish nationality and Kingdom.

And not only so, but I challenge anyone to deny, that when the 139 texts of the N.T. that mention the Kingdom of God (or of heaven) are taken in their natural sense, which is the sense in which they have been understood by every Bible teacher and Bible reader for nineteen centuries, they are all found to be in perfect harmony with the prophecy we are now considering, and which is quoted and applied by Paul. Whereas, on the other hand, it is utterly impossible (as I propose now to show) by any torturing and twisting of the language employed, to make a number of the plainest of those 139 texts do anything but conflict palpably with the teachings of modern dispensationalism.

How then, it will be asked, does the "Scofield Bible" maintain its doctrine concerning God's Kingdom? How does it deal with those 139 references thereto in the N.T.? This brings us to one of the most astonishing features of the strange affair we are now examining.

In the introductory pages of the "Scofield Bible" the promise is given that by "A new system of topical references all the greater truths of the divine revelation are traced through the entire Bible from the first mention to the last"; and also that its "summaries" are analytic of "the whole teaching of Scripture."

We are now about to inquire how this fair promise has been carried out with respect to one of the very greatest of "the greater truths of the divine revelation"--that concerning the Kingdom of God. And briefly the distressing fact in this regard is that (as pointed out by Mr. Thomas Bolton of Australia, in a leaflet on The Kingdom of God) whereas the Kingdom is mentioned in seventeen of the Books of the N.T., the "Scofield Bible" cites only five of those Books; and whereas the Kingdom is mentioned 139 times by name, only 21 of the verses are cited in the "Scofield Bible," the other 118 being totally ignored!

It would be quite in order, doubtless, to ask if this is dealing fairly and keeping faith with the thousands who have purchased this new "Bible." But without pressing that inquiry, I hasten to direct the reader's attention to a few of the 118 references to the Kingdom that are found in God's Bible, but which are passed over in silence by the "Scofield Bible," despite the promise that it would be "traced through the entire Bible, from the first mention to the last." And I leave it to the intelligent reader to say whether under the circumstances of the case, those particular texts could have been ignored by editor and co-editors for any other reason than that they manifestly cannot be made to agree with, or do anything but flatly to contradict, the new postponement theory.

To begin with let us refer to Matt. 18:3; 19:14; Mark 10:14, 15; Luke 18:16, 17. Here is teaching concerning the Kingdom from the lips of Christ Himself, teaching which is so important that it is given in three of the Gospels. And this is the substance of it:

"Verily I say unto you, Except ye be converted, and become as little children, ye shall not enter into the Kingdom of Heaven" (Mat. 18:3).

Suffer little children, and forbid them not, to come unto Me; for of such is the Kingdom of heaven" (id. 19:14). "But when Jesus saw it He was much displeased, and said unto them, Suffer the little children to come unto Me, and forbid them not; for of such is the Kingdom of God" (Mark 10:14).

Verily I say unto you, Whosoever shall not receive the Kingdom of God as a little child, shall in no wise enter therein" (Luke 18:17).

These passages plainly declare the vital truth that, in order to be saved, one must "be converted," and become as a little child; that is to say, he must become a new creature in Christ Jesus. And the parallel expressions in the context "enter into life" (Mat. 18:8, 9) show that to enter into the Kingdom of God, and into life, are the same thing. Moreover, when, in the same chapter of Mark, Christ said "It is easier for a camel to go through the eye of a needle, than for a rich man to enter into the Kingdom of God" (v. 25), it is recorded that "They were astonished out of measure, saying among themselves, WHO THEN CAN BE SAVED" (v. 26). And the next verse shows they were right in their understanding that to enter into the Kingdom meant to be saved; for it is written: "And Jesus looking upon them saith, With men it is impossible, but not with God; for with God all things are possible" (v. 27).

Beyond question then, in the light of these Scriptures, the Kingdom of God, referred to scores of times in our Lord's preaching and teaching, and which indeed is far the most prominent subject thereof, is not the earthly Kingdom of Jewish hopes, but that heavenly realm that is entered only upon individual repentance and faith, and only by the door of the new birth.

By a comparison of the above texts, and of many other passages that are common to the three synoptic Gospels, it will be clearly seen that the phrases, "Kingdom of heaven" and "Kingdom of God" are used interchangeably.

Furthermore it should be noted in connection with these particular texts that they flatly contradict the teaching of the Scofield Bible to the effect that the offer of the Kingdom had been "morally rejected" by the Jews at the time of the events recorded in Matt. XI (note on Mat. 11:20); and that at that point began "the new message of Jesus--not the Kingdom, but rest and service." But the truth in this connection is that the subject of the Kingdom occupied the same place of prominence in our Lord's public teaching down to the day of His death; and that after His resurrection He remained forty days on earth, being seen of His disciples, "and speaking of the things pertaining to the kingdom of God" (Act 1:3).

Matthew 23:13 is a specially illuminating scripture, one that is decisive as to whether the Kingdom of God had been withdrawn and postponed or not. It is fatal to editor Scofield's theory, and it is ignored in his treatment of the subject.

The occasion was our Lord's last public discourse; and it is worthy of note that, as His first public discourse, the Sermon on the Mount began with seven beatitudes pronounced upon His disciples, so the last began with seven woes pronounced upon the scribes and Pharisees. Let us compare the first of each series:

"Blessed are the poor in spirit; for their's is the Kingdom of heaven" (Matt. 5:3).

"But woe unto you, scribes and Pharisees, hypocrites! for ye shut up the Kingdom of heaven against men; for ye neither go in yourselves, neither suffer ye them that are entering to go in" (Matt. 23:13).

There is much and valuable truth to be learned from the last quoted text, but I am now citing it because of the transparently clear testimony it bears to the fact that the Kingdom of heaven, of which Christ had spoken in His Sermon on the Mount, and which had been the main subject of His teaching, had not been postponed, as the Scofield Bible unequivocally states. For here our Lord addresses the scribes and Pharisees, pronouncing a woe upon them because they were at that very time shutting up the Kingdom of heaven against men; they were not entering in themselves, and they suffered not them that were entering to go in. Beyond all question therefore, the Kingdom was then present, for some were actually "entering in."

But why were the Jewish leaders refusing to go in themselves? and how were they hindering others from entering? By their doctrine. For the corner stone of their creed was the very same doctrine that has lately been dug up out of the pit of false Judaism and has been made the cornerstone of modern dispensationalism. They were not going in themselves, and they were preventing others from entering, because they held and taught that the Kingdom of heaven, the reign of Messiah which the prophets of Israel had foretold, was a Jewish and an earthly affair, not a spiritual and a heavenly kingdom.

Seeing then the disastrous effect of that doctrine upon the learned rabbis, the leaders of the most orthodox sect of the Jews, have we not the gravest reason to be fearful of the consequences, now that the same doctrine is held and zealously propagated by learned leaders of the most orthodox party in Christendom in our time? For it was not the Sadducees--the materialists and modernists of those days--who taught the deadly error, but the Pharisees, the "fundamentalists" of that period.

And how does it work now? If to be saved is to be in the Kingdom of God, as we have just shown by our Lord's own teaching, and as Paul also plainly taught (Col. 1:13), and if there be now no Kingdom of God for men to enter, how shall they be saved? Is there anything in "modernism" that is worse than this? And can the "Fundamentalists" of our time expect to prevail in their conflict with the "Modernists," so long as they harbor, and are even zealous for, a brand of modernism that certainly is more modern, and in some respects more pernicious, than that they are combatting? Hearken, my Fundamentalist brethren; you must do some thorough house-cleaning on your own premises before you can undertake, with any prospect of success, to put the large Christian household in order.

Attention has already been called to the statement of Christ, recorded in Luke 16:16. "The law and the prophets were until John; since that time the Kingdom of God is preached, and every man presseth into it."

Those who have no theory to defend, but who sincerely desire to know by the Word of the Lord just when the change in God's dealings took place (or, to use the modern phraseology, when the change of dispensation occurred) could ask nothing more to the point or more satisfactory than this. For here we have Christ's own word for it that the new era began with the preaching and baptism of John; and further that what properly characterizes that new era is the preaching of the Kingdom of God. This text shows also that the preaching of the gospel of the Kingdom had not ceased at the time those words were spoken. For the Lord's statement was that "since that time the Kingdom of God is preached, and every man presseth into it."

So here is another text that is sufficient in itself to prove that the Kingdom had not at that time been postponed. Is it not a significant fact then that this particularly illuminating Scripture also was ignored by editor Scofield in the process of tracing the subject of the Kingdom of God "through the entire Bible, from the first mention to the last?"

Passing on to the next chapter of Luke we come to another text which surely has a strong claim upon the attention of those who are seeking the teaching of the Word of God upon the subject of His Kingdom. Our Lord was then on His way to Jerusalem to die there. "And when He was demanded of the Pharisees when the Kingdom of God should come, He answered them and said, The Kingdom of God cometh not with observation; neither shall they say, Lo here! or Lo there! for behold, the kingdom of God is within you" (Luke 17:20, 21).

This is illuminating indeed. First, our Lord was answering what was in the hearts of those (the Pharisees) who put the question to Him; their doctrine being that the Kingdom of God would come (when it did come) with the accompaniment of outward displays of Divine power, whereby the enemies of the Jews would be miraculously overwhelmed, and they themselves be swept triumphantly into, and securely established in, the coveted place of world supremacy. So he corrected their error by saying that the Kingdom of God came not with ocular evidence, which is the literal meaning of the word rendered "observation" in other words it was not the sort of kingdom they were expecting. And the verb He used was in the present tense, "cometh"; which makes it plain that He was speaking of the manner in which the Kingdom of God was coming at that time. This is what we are specially seeking to determine just now. And He proceeded to emphasize these facts by adding that there would be nothing of a startling or sensational character, such as would cause the spectators to say "Look here! Look yonder!" "For"--and now, being about to say something He wished specially to impress upon them, He uses an impressive word--"behold, the kingdom of God is within you." Some prefer the marginal reading, "among you"; but the sense is the same. The Kingdom was in existence at that time. It "is." But it was a spiritual Kingdom, such as could not be discerned by the natural eye. This agrees with what Paul afterwards said about it; that its sphere of being was "in the Holy Ghost" (Rom. 14:17).

The Kingdom of God is mentioned three times in the Gospel of John; and the statements of Christ there recorded concerning it are of supreme importance; yet they are all ignored in the Scofield Bible. Why?

The third chapter of John is the best known chapter, and the sixteenth verse thereof is the best known verse, in the Bible. But is it not commonly overlooked in reading it, that the subject of the chapter is the Kingdom of God? The whole land had been aroused by the preaching of John the Baptist, and all were in a state of keenest expectation because of his proclamation that the Kingdom of God was at hand. Therefore, whatever teaching was given by the Lord at that period (before the commencement of His own preaching, which did not begin until after John had been cast into prison, Mark 1:14) has special value for the purpose of our present inquiry, since it tells us what the phrase, "Kingdom of God," meant in the preaching of John.1 How significant, therefore, that the Holy Spirit has made note of the fact that, at the time of our Lord's conversation with Nicodemus, John was baptizing; and that He adds, "For John was not yet cast into prison" (vv. 23, 24)

And it is of the utmost significance that the very first words of our Lord to that "teacher of Israel" strike directly at the cardinal error of rabbinism--the doctrine that the Kingdom of God is of earthly and Jewish character. For He said, and with all the tremendous emphasis of His double Amen, "Verily, verily, I say unto thee, Except a man be born again, he cannot see the Kingdom of God" (v. 3); and "Verily, verily, I say unto thee, Except a man be born of water, and of the Spirit, he cannot enter into the Kingdom of God" (v. 5).

Here is truly "fundamental" truth concerning the Kingdom of God, truth that was delivered along with the very first preaching of that Kingdom. Natural descent from Abraham does not insure entrance into the Kingdom of God, as erroneously taught by the rabbis then and by the dispensationalists now. To enter into that Kingdom a man must be born of the Spirit. And the next words of Christ emphasize this fundamental truth: "that which is born of the flesh"--whether of Abraham or any other man--"is flesh; and that which is born of the Spirit is spirit" (v. 6). John also in his teaching gave prominence to this truth; for he warned the Pharisees and Sadducees who came to his baptism, saying: "Think not to say within yourselves, We have Abraham to our father; for I say unto you, that God is able of these stones to raise up children unto Abraham" (Mat. 3:9). For the natural descendants of Abraham came from the dust of the ground, as did all the children of Adam; but none can enter the Kingdom of God without "the washing of regeneration and renewing of the Holy Ghost" (Tit. 3:5).

Further our Lord's word to Nicodemus declared plainly that God had sent His Son into the world (not to set up, or even to offer, a Jewish Kingdom, but) to save "THE WORLD" (v. 17). He revealed to him that, "As Moses lifted up the serpent in the wilderness, even so must the Son of man be lifted up; that whosoever"--whether Jew or Gentile--"believeth in Him should not perish, but have eternal life" (v. 15) ; and that He had come--not in fulfilment of some supposed promise to give national glory to the Jews, but--because "God so loved THE WORLD, that He gave His only begotten Son, that WHOSOEVER believeth in Him should not perish, but have everlasting life" (v. 16).

These verses clearly reveal, and all Scripture is in perfect agreement (of course), that the Kingdom of God is (and was then, and ever will be) that spiritual realm in which the authority of God's "King eternal" (I Tim. 1:17) Jesus Christ risen from the dead, is acknowledged, and His law "obeyed from the heart" (Rom. 6:17) by a people who have believed on His name, have been washed in His blood, and have been regenerated by the Holy Ghost.

These are the first two references to the Kingdom in John's Gospel. The third mention thereof is also of the utmost significance; and it likewise furnishes a complete refutation of what was taught by the rabbis then and by the dispensationalists now. It is found in Christ's testimony on His own behalf before Pilate. The words are plain enough; but in order to get their full force, and to perceive their direct bearing upon the question we are examining, it is needful to have in mind that the crime of which the Lord was accused before Pilate, the local representative of Caesar, was sedition, and specifically that He was proposing to set up another kingdom, in opposition to that of Caesar; "Saying that He Himself is Christ a King" (Luke 23:1; John 19:12, 15). As to this accusation, our Lord when asked by Pilate the direct question, "art thou the King of the Jews?" replied, "Thou sayest it" (Mark 15:2), which is an emphatic "Yes." But, as John's record shows, He testified nevertheless that He had not been guilty of sedition against Caesar, because the Kingdom He had proclaimed was one that did not conflict with Caesar's. In fact it did not even belong to this world. These are His words:

"Jesus answered, My Kingdom is not of this world, if My Kingdom were of this world, then would my servants fight that I should not be delivered to the Jews; but now is my Kingdom not from hence." (John 18: 36).

Think what the teaching of the Scofield Bible does by implication to this simple, plain and all-important word of Christ, which it passes by in silence! For, by that teaching, this testimony of our Lord, given in open court when on trial for His life, was not true. According to that teaching the Kingdom He had been proclaiming both in person and also by the lips of His disciples throughout the length and breadth of the land, was of this world; and its establishment would necessarily have involved the overthrow of Caesar's dominion, and the subjugation of the whole world to the Jewish nation. How then can we account for it that this text is ignored in the notes of the Scofield Bible? And let it be remembered in this connection that when the Pharisees had previously attempted to entrap the Lord into some utterance which they could use against Him as savoring of sedition again Caesar, He perceived their hypocrisy and expressly commanded them to "Render unto Caesar the things which are Caesar's, and unto God, the things that are God's" (Mat. 22:17-21). For the Kingdom of God is not in anywise antagonistic to the kingdoms and rulers of this world. On the contrary, the law of Christ commands loyalty to them, because "the powers that be are ordained of God" (Rom. 13 :1) ; and it requires of all the citizens of His Kingdom that they submit themselves "to every ordinance of man for the Lord's sake" (I Pet. 2:13).

The last verses of Acts give a parting view of the apostle Paul. They tell us that he dwelt two whole years in his own hired house (in Rome), where he "received all that came in unto him, preaching the Kingdom of God, and teaching those things which concern the Lord Jesus Christ" (Acts 28:30, 31). Evidently Paul had not heard that the preaching of the Kingdom of God did not belong to this "dispensation." For in those days there was no "Scofield Bible" to enlighten him. On the other hand, we are not informed as to how this passage can be reconciled with modern dispensationalism, for the Scofield Bible ignores it.

Romans 14:17, which I have already quoted, merits special attention; for it is the text that gives God's own definition of His Kingdom; and for that reason it is the very last verse we should expect to find omitted from any summary that purports to give the teaching of the Scriptures on the subject of that Kingdom. This is the passage:

"For the Kingdom of God is not meat and drink" (more literally, not eating and drinking) "but righteousness and peace and joy in the Holy Ghost."

The Kingdom is here defined both negatively and positively. We are told first what it is not, and then what it is; and hence the text is the more enlightening for our present purpose. For a contrast is here presented between the Kingdom of God and the historical Kingdom of David, which the rabbinists supposed (as the dispensationalists do flow) were one and the same. Concerning the kingdom of David it is recorded that they who came to make him king "were with David three days, eating and drinking", and that those who lived in the territory of the other Tribes, even unto Issachar, and Zebulon and Naphthali, brought bread on asses, and on camels, and on mules, and on oxen; also meat, meal, cakes of figs, and bunches of raisins, and wine, and oil, and oxen and sheep abundantly; for there was joy in Israel" (I Chr. 12:39, 40). Also it is written that David in those days "dealt to every one of Israel, both man and woman, to every one a loaf of bread, and a good piece of flesh, and a flagon of wine." (Id. 16:3).

But the Kingdom of God is not like that. Everyone in that Kingdom has (1) the righteousness of God, has (2) peace with God, and has (3) joy in the Holy Ghost. And it is worthy of note that Paul is here summarizing the blessings of the Gospel, as he had already stated then in chapter 5. For there is declared the fundamental doctrine that (1) being justified (made righteous) by faith, we have (2) peace with God through our Lord Jesus"...and not only so, but (3) "we also joy in God" (Rom 5:1, 11). The blessings of the Kingdom of God are not the fruits of the land of Canaan, but the fruits of the Holy Spirit; and the "joy" that was in Israel because of the good things to eat and drink, is replaced by "joy in the Holy Ghost." This is "the Gospel of the Kingdom," as preached and taught by Paul.

It is a cause for profound astonishment that, in what purports to be a complete setting forth of the teaching of Scripture as to the Kingdom of God, this particular text (Rom. 14:17) should have been ignored; since it has the unique distinction of giving the Holy Spirit's own definition of that Kingdom.

I come now to what I regard as the strongest of all the testimonies concerning the Kingdom of God that we have by the pen of the apostle Paul. It is found in the first chapter of Colossians; and it is ignored in the Scofield Bible. Paul is there speaking of "the word of the truth of the gospel" (v. 5) and of the fruit it brought forth in them and others; mention being made of their "faith in Christ Jesus," of "the hope" laid up for them in heaven, and of their "love to all the saints. Here are faith, hope, and love; these three. And he goes on to exhort them as to "Giving thanks to the Father, Who hath made us meet to be partakers of the inheritance of the saints in light; Who hath delivered us from the power of darkness, and hath translated us into the Kingdom of His dear Son; in Whom we have redemption through His blood, even the forgiveness of sins" (vv. 12-14).

Here is proof positive that, not only did the Kingdom of God's dear Son exist in Paul's day, and had not been postponed, but that it is something that is vital to our salvation. Clearly, if there be no Kingdom of God there is no gospel, and no salvation. The passage agrees in all essential points with the teaching that Christ gave to Nicodemus. For it reveals redemption for all "the world" as the purpose for which God sent forth His Son, and the bringing into existence of the Kingdom of Christ, in which those who enter by faith in Him are born of God and know Him as "Father" (the Spirit being mentioned in verse 8).

This passage in Colossians also throws light upon the words quoted in an earlier chapter from Mark's Gospel: "The beginning of the gospel of Jesus Christ, the Son of God";..."The time is fulfilled, and the kingdom of God is at hand; repent ye, and believe the gospel" (Mark 1:1, 15). This tells us that "the gospel" is that of "Jesus Christ the Son of God"; and Paul in Colossians declares the word of the truth of the gospel to be that God the Father hath translated us into the kingdom of His dear Son.

We might pursue this branch of our inquiry much further, and with profit. But enough has been said to indicate what the reader might expect to find in the way of valuable instruction concerning the Kingdom by examination of the more than a hundred other references in the N.T. to that subject which, like those briefly examined above, are ignored in the Scofield Bible.

Notes

1. For it is to be noted that the dispensationalists, in their effort to make the Epistles (and also the later part of the Gospels) agree with their theory have resorted to the strange expedient of saying that the phrase "Kingdom of God" meant the Kingdom of Jewish hopes at first, but after it was "rejected," and "withdrawn," the term was used with a different meaning. Of course, no proof in support of this is cited; for there is none.

Chapter Six - The Gospels: to What "Dispensation" Do They Belong?

I HAVE sought to show in the preceding pages that the Kingdom of God which was the subject of Christ's preaching and teaching is just what all Christians have understood it to be until recent times, that is, a purely spiritual realm; and further that it had not been postponed when His parting words to His disciples were spoken (Acts 1:3). I do not see how any testimonies as to this could possibly be clearer or stronger than those we have cited from all the four Gospels; or how, in the light of our Lord's own words, there can be any question that the long accepted Christian doctrine as to the true Israel and as to the Kingdom foretold by the prophets, is founded squarely upon Christ's own teaching. Yet the "Scofield Bible" asserts (in its "Introduction to the Gospels") that the long accepted views of Christ's followers concerning those supremely important subjects, were not derived from His teaching, but were "a legacy in Protestant thought from post-Apostolic and Roman Catholic theology."

The statements in this note are so radical, and they involve matters of such superlative importance to all mankind, that I purpose now to give them a thorough examination in the light of the Old Testament, as well as in that of the New. For those statements raise a question both as to "the Old Testament foreview of the Kingdom," and also as to what Kingdom it was that Jesus Christ announced as at hand.

But before undertaking that examination, there is something that should be said as to the truly calamitous effects of such a "note" as that just referred to (quoted more fully below) when placed at the forefront of the Gospels. It is a specimen of the means whereby it is sought to fabricate a semblance of support for the novel and exceedingly pernicious doctrine that the life and ministry of our Lord belong not to this era of grace, to "these last days" in which God has "spoken unto us by His Son" (Heb. 1:1, 2), but-- to the era of law; and that the commandments of God the Father spoken by Jesus Christ (specially the Sermon on the Mount) pertain--not to those who are saved by grace now, but--to the Jewish people, a reconstituted earthly nation of a yet future "dispensation."

In view of the peculiarly tender affection with which the Lord's people, throughout the centuries of our era, have regarded the four Gospels, and of the fact that those particular parts of the Word of God have ever been specially cherished by all the household of faith, it is a mystery indeed, one of the greatest of "the mysteries of the Kingdom," how this new doctrine, which takes away from the redeemed people of God their priceless treasurers, and relegates them to a conjectural future generation of "Israel after all flesh," has ever found even a foothold among them. [1]

We will now take notice of the way the Gospels are handled in the notes of the Scofield Bible with the intent to make an opening for the new doctrine we are examining. That publication, in its "Introduction to the Gospels," says:

"In approaching the study of the Gospels the mind should be freed, so far as possible from mere theological concepts and presuppositions. Especially is it necessary to exclude the notion--a legacy in Protestant thought from post-Apostolic and Roman Catholic theology--that the church is the true Israel, and that the Old Testament foreview of the kingdom is fulfilled in the church."

First we have here what appears to be merely a general word of caution; namely, that "in approaching the study of the Gospels," we should free our minds "from mere theological concepts and pre-suppositions." This seems reasonable enough; for who would dispute that it were well to have our minds freed from mere theological concepts, not only "when approaching the study of the Gospels," but at all times?

But Dr. Scofield was not concerned, when he penned the above words, with "theological concepts and presuppositions" in general. For his aim plainly was to cast discredit upon the view always held by the household of faith touching the Kingdom of God the Gospel of God and the Words of Jesus Christ, and to introduce in its stead a new doctrine radically different therefrom.

The editor of the Scofield Bible was aware, of course, that the great theme of the Gospels is the Kingdom of God; for that is evident to the most careless reader, and further he must have known that, from the very beginning of the Christian era it had been accepted as indisputable truth that, not only the prophecies concerning the glorious reign of David's promised Son, but also the announcements by John the Baptist and Christ

Himself that the Kingdom of heaven was at hand, had their realization and fulfilment in that Kingdom of God's dear Son, into which those who are saved through faith in Jesus Christ are forthwith translated (Col. 1:12, 13). He must have known it to be the universal, age-long, and elemental teaching of christianity, that the Kingdom foretold by the prophets, and that announced by the Lord and His forerunner, was realized in the blessed company of those who are called and saved through the Gospel of Jesus Christ. And since it was the editor's purpose to introduce to his readers a kingdom-doctrine "diverse" from the above, and "strange" to christian ears, he must needs begin by an attempt to discredit and to shake their confidence in the long established and universally accepted christian doctrine of the Kingdom of God. This he proceeds to do in the two sentences quoted above.

The first sentence deals in generalities, the obvious intent being to create suspicion of the accepted teaching by referring to it contemptuously as a "mere theological concept." The second sentence, however, is quite explicit. Here the accepted doctrine of the kingdom is termed a "notion"; and the assertion is boldly made that it is "necessary to exclude" it. Why "necessary"? For no other reason, so far as appears, than that it stands squarely in the way of the new doctrine the editor and those of his way of thinking have undertaken to propagate. We do not question in the least that their intentions are good, their motives pure, and their purposes sincere. But that does not make their doctrine any the less a startling innovation and a dangerous heresy. Most certainly it is "necessary to exclude" either that doctrine concerning the Kingdom of God which all christians have held from the beginning of the gospel era, or else to, exclude this new doctrine that is now offered as a substitute; for there is irreconcilable antagonism between them. It is some satisfaction to me that Dr. Scofield recognized this; for it makes quite evident that a sharp issue has been raised, and that a choice must be made between the two conflicting views.

But now we come to a more serious matter. For the assertion is made that this "notion" is--not properly a part of true Protestant doctrine at all, but merely--"a legacy in Protestant thought from post-apostolic and Roman Catholic theology."

Here is a statement of fact; but one for which not a scrap of evidence has ever been produced, and for which, I confidently declare, not a scrap of evidence exists. The history of christian doctrine continues in an unbroken line from apostolic times to our day; and if it had been possible to produce from the copious writings of the "Church fathers," any proof that the doctrine concerning the Kingdom of God taught by the Scofield Bible and by certain Bible Schools of our day was ever held by christians, real or nominal, in times past, it would have been produced long ago; seeing that the present writer and not a few others have been challenging this new doctrine, and largely upon the score of its entire novelty, for ten years past.

My first answer therefore, to the above quoted statement is that it is not true; and that on the contrary the teaching here referred to as a "notion," and as a legacy from post-apostolic theology is the teaching of the New Testament itself, and has been the teaching also of sound and evangelical teachers and expositors of the Bible from the days of the Apostles to the latter part of the nineteenth century.

Furthermore, the assertion in the above quotation from the Scofield Bible that what is therein termed a notion is a legacy from "Roman Catholic theology" is an evil mixture of innuendo and misrepresentation. If it were true that Roman Catholic theology teaches the same doctrine of the Kingdom of God that has been accepted heretofore by all evangelical christians, that fact would be not at all to the discredit of the doctrine itself. It would be just as fair and just as reasonable to attempt to cast discredit upon the doctrine of the Deity of Christ, or that of His bodily resurrection, or that of the inspiration of the Scriptures, by pointing to the fact that Rome has given a place to those

doctrines in her theology.

But the truth of the matter is that the Romish doctrine of the Kingdom, in the respects wherein it differs from the accepted Protestant doctrine, presents a striking resemblance to ancient rabbinism and to modern dispensationalism. For the essential feature of each of those three systems of error is that "the Old Testament foreview of the Kingdom" was a Kingdom of earthly character. In respect to that cardinal feature of the great kingdom heresy, Judaism, Dispensationalism, and Romanism are all in perfect agreement. Where they differ among themselves is that the first two say the earthly Kingdom foretold by the prophets was to be Jewish, and the last says it was to be Romish--and as between those two variant views it makes little difference, to my mind, which is preferred.

And not only is the new "dispensational teaching" in accord with both Judaism and Romanism in holding the Kingdom of God to be of earthly character, but it is, in respect to another of its distinctive features, closely akin to another great heresy of today, Russellism. For the outstanding doctrine of the latter it that, following this gospel-era, there is to be another "dispensation" (the Millennium) in which salvation is to be on a wholesale scale. Dispensationalism does not go to the length of teaching that there is to be universal salvation in a coming day; but it comes dangerously close to it. For it avers that every person of Jewish descent is to be saved; [2] and that they will be constituted into a nation on earth.

And further it is sometimes expressly taught by dispensationalists, and always is implied in their doctrine, that there will then be other saved nations (and indeed none but saved nations) in the world; for it is a prominent feature of this teaching that the Jews are to be the chief of the nations, and in some sense are to exercise authority over all the nations on earth. So this comes, I say, dangerously close to Russellism.

But if there be any truth at all in this doctrine of abounding salvation in a coming day, it is clear that the apostle Paul did greatly err in saying, "Behold, NOW is the day of salvation" (2 Cor. 6:2); for that designation would justly belong to the coming Millennium.

I expect to return to this subject in a subsequent chapter.

Notes

1. The very day after the writing of the above paragraph came a letter from a missionary in Africa in which he declared his conviction that a great many of the Lord's people "are suffering from a lack of application of the truths of our Lord's Ministry, in the Gospels, to their daily lives." And he said that men of God among "Brethren" (naming George Mueller and Robert Chapman) "owed their fruitfulness, and the long continued influence of their ministry, to the emphasis they laid upon 'following Christ' in accordance with His utterances that are now so frequently relegated to 'another dispensation'."
2. Citing as a proof text, among others, Romans 11:26, "And so all Israel shall be saved."

Chapter Seven - The Kingdom "at Hand." - The Order of Revelation

THE notes of the Scofield Bible on the subjects of the Kingdom leave us at Matthew 16 with the statement that the old testimony was ended and the new not yet ready. There the all-important subject of the Kingdom was dropped, so far as the notes are concerned, and our Lord is left without any message at all. We suspect the reason for this is that human ingenuity could go no further. For how, on the editor's theory, could the words of Mark 1:1--"The beginning of the gospel of Jesus Christ the Son of God"--be explained? Or the Lord's words, "The time is fulfilled, and the Kingdom of God is at hand. Repent ye and believe the gospel" (Mark 1:14-15)? Or the fact that Paul everywhere "preached the kingdom of God," and that he witnessed "both to small and great, saying none other things than those which the prophets and Moses did say should come" (Acts 20:25; 26:22)? Or the fact that God has "translated us into the

56

Kingdom of His dear Son" (Col. 1:13)? It is only because of the impossibility of making these and other important Scripture fit in with the editor's theory that we can explain the remarkable fact that he has passed them by without a word of comment. The users of this edition must have wondered at this strange silence.

Those readers must also have been puzzled and disappointed at the notes on Acts 13-6. In the text we have the important statement that the Lord, after His resurrection, was seen of the apostles forty days, during which He was "speaking of things pertaining to the Kingdom of God." This, of course, could only mean that He was instructing them concerning the work of that Kingdom in which they were to serve Him so soon as they should receive power through the coming of the Holy Spirit, Whom He at that very time promised to send upon them. For why should the Lord be giving them at that time directions concerning a kingdom which had been withdrawn and postponed? Surely an explanation is demanded; but all that is offered in the note is this singular comment: "doubtless, according to His custom (Lu. 24:27, 32, 44, 45) teaching them out of the Scriptures." Obviously this comment does not explain the text, but contradicts it. The passage itself needs no explanation, for it is transparently clear. But this is one of "the hard places" for the editor's theory, which goes to pieces on this one passage. "Helps" indeed are needed; but the note merely exposes the erroneous nature of the theory. If the Lord was "teaching them out of the Scriptures," and not giving them fresh revelations and instructions, then certainly "the Scriptures" from which He was "teaching them" must have had to do with the Kingdom of God; for we have the express statement of verse 3 that that is what He was instructing them about. And since the very Scriptures which the editor cites in the above note had to do with the Lord's sufferings and death and resurrection, as declared in Luke XXIV, then the Lord's death and resurrection, and also the coming of the Holy Spirit, must needs have preceded the Kingdom of God. That is indeed the simple truth of the matter, and every pertinent Scripture is in perfect agreement therewith. Hence the Kingdom of God preached by the Lord from the beginning of His ministry could not have been the restoring of the earthly kingdom of Israel.

The notes to which we have referred show very plainly just where the editor has missed his way in attempting to trace the order of the fulfilment of Old Testament prophecy and promise. The editor comes to the New Testament with the very novel and radical "theological concept and presupposition" that the Kingdom or era of blessing foretold by the prophets of Israel was the earthly Kingdom of Jewish expectancy; and that the appointed time for it in God's plan of the ages, was at the first coming of Christ. For the editor says: "When Christ appeared to the Jewish people, the next thing, in the order of revelation as it then stood, should have been the setting up of the Davidic kingdom (Mat. 4:17)." This is a crucial statement; but it is very easy to show that it is quite erroneous. We have only to look back as far as the last verses of the Old Testament to see that" the next thing in the order of revelation as it then stood" was the ministry of a special messenger who should prepare the way of the Lord by turning many of the children of Israel to the Lord their God, lest He should come and "smite the earth with a curse." We know, moreover, that the turning of many Israelites to the Lord is exactly what did take place (Lu. 1:13-17); and we know also that, but for John's Elijah-like ministry, the earth would have been smitten with a curse (Mal. 4:6). John's ministry was therefore indispensably necessary as an introduction to the predicted era of blessing, which era he announced when he said: "the kingdom of heaven is at hand."

What kingdom then was it that the Lord Himself thus proclaimed as "at hand," and which He called "the Kingdom of Heaven" and "Kingdom of God"? Did the Lord from heaven come personally to proclaim with His own lips a Kingdom "at hand" which was not at hand? Did He call upon those who heard Him to "believe" what was not true? And did those who did believe Him have to learn later on that they had been deceived, and that the Kingdom which He positively declared to be at hand was postponed? They who hold with the editor of the "Scofield" Bible would have to say "Yes" to these questions. For though there was a Kingdom then at hand, and though its divinely given name is "the Kingdom of God" (Acts 8:12; Rom. 14:17, etc.), these modern teachers tell us that the Kingdom of God which was at hand is not the Kingdom of God which the Lord, Who knoweth all things and Who cannot lie, said to be at hand; but that the Kingdom of God which He positively declared as at hand, was some other "Kingdom of God" which was not at hand at all. Is it possible, I ask in all seriousness, to do greater violence than this to the statements of the Lord?

But let us see how this simple and transparently clear announcement of the Lord is made to square with the editor's novel doctrine; for we have here an exceedingly interesting and instructive example of the methods by which the postponement theory is upheld. For, as we shall now see, it was needful to the maintenance of that theory, that the meaning of a common Bible phrase should be completely changed; and accordingly the needed change is wrought through the instrumentality of one of the editor's notes, which contains the following assertion:

"'At hand' is never a positive affirmation that the person or thing said to be 'at hand' will immediately appear, but only that no known or predicted event must intervene. When Christ appeared to the Jewish people, the next thing in the order of revelation as it then stood should have been the setting up of the Davidic kingdom" (italics ours).

Is any proof offered in support of this statement? Not a word; though if true it would be easy to establish it by citing a few passages which would show the Biblical usage of the phrase. Now, what are the facts as to the usage of this phrase in the New Testament? The word here used by our Lord and here translated "at hand" is used by Himself and by the inspired writers of the Gospels and Acts over fifty times, and in every instance it is just what the editor says it never is namely, a "positive affirmation" that the person or thing said to be "at hand" was at hand. In other words, the statement of the editor is exactly the reverse of the truth. This is easily shown.

The word referred to is usually translated "is (or is come) near, or nigh"; and we will give a few of the more than fifty occurrences of that word in the Gospels and Acts.

Mat. 21:1 "When they drew nigh unto Jerusalem."

This means that they were nigh to Jerusalem; and so in every other case.

21:34 "'When the time of the fruit drew nigh."

24:32 "Ye know that summer is nigh."

24:33 "When ye shall see these things, know that it is near."

Mk. 2:4 "Could not come nigh unto Him for the press."

Lu. 7:12 "When He came nigh to the gate.

15:1 "Then drew near unto Him all the publicans and sinners for to hear Him."

18:35 "As He was come nigh unto Jericho."

19:11 "Because He was nigh to Jerusalem."

22:1 "The feast of unleavened bread drew nigh."

22:47 "Judas drew near unto Jesus to kiss Him."

John 2:13 "The Jews' passover was at hand."

6:4 "A feast of the Jews was nigh."

7:2 'The Jews' feast of tabernacles was at hand."

6:19 "And drew nigh unto the ship."

It is evident that in all these cases the word which our Lord used repeatedly in proclaiming the Kingdom of God as "at hand," means close by, near, about to come or be reached. In fact it is the most appropriate word that could be chosen for expressing the very idea for which the editor says it is never used.

On several occasions in speaking of the Kingdom of God the Lord used even a stronger word than "is at hand." Thus, in Matthew 12:28 He said: "But if I cast out devils by the Spirit of God, then the Kingdom of God is come unto you." Here the Lord declared that the Kingdom was actually present. So likewise in Luke 17:20, 21 He said (speaking to the Pharisees): "For behold, the Kingdom of God is within (i.e. in the midst of) you." [1] In both these cases He referred to Himself as constituting God's Kingdom at that time; that is to say, He Himself was the realm in which God's will was being done in the power of the Holy Ghost. Still later, again speaking to the Pharisees, and long after the kingdom had been, on the editor's theory, withdrawn, the Lord said: "But woe unto you Scribes and Pharisees, hypocrites, for ye shut up the Kingdom of heaven against men; for ye neither go in yourselves, neither suffer ye them that are entering to go in" (Mat. 23:13).

In the foregoing comments we have referred only to the use of the expressions "at hand" and "come nigh" in the Gospels; for it is in them that the announcement of the era which actually was at hand would be found. It is attempted sometimes to force a different meaning on the words "at hand" (or rather to reverse their meaning completely) because of the fact that in Romans 13:12 Paul says, "the day is at hand," and in Philippians 4:5 he says "the Lord is at hand." It is assumed, of course, that both these statements refer to the second coming of Christ. But it seems quite clear that "the day" to which Paul refers is the day that had dawned then, i.e. at the first coming of Christ. For he says it is "now high time to awake out of sleep"; and because the day has dawned he exhorts us to cast off the works of darkness and to put on the armour of light. We believe the sense is the same as in 1 John 2:8, "the darkness is passing away and the true light is already shining" (Gr.).

In Philippians 4:5 there is no reference to the Lord's coming, but to the fact that He is always "near" to supply the needs of His people.

In the foot-note last quoted above, is a crucial statement the settlement of which will decide the whole matter in dispute. The assertion is that "When Christ appeared to the Jewish people, the next thing, in the order of revelation as it then stood, should have been the setting up of the Davidic kingdom." Again we call attention to the absence of any attempt whatever to support this assertion by proof; and also to the implication that the "order of revelation" is a changeable thing. For it is plainly implied that the order of revelation might be something different at another time.

"As it then stood" the next thing was "the Davidic Kingdom"--at least so says the editor. But if so, what prevented the order of Divine revelation from proceeding? If the Davidic kingdom was then in order in God's plan, what prevented its coming into existence? According to the same authority (for no other is cited), the explanation is that the Jews of Christ's day would not accept it.

This is stupefying. Is the order of revelation of God's purposes such an uncertain thing that the opposition of carnal men can set it aside? If, when God's "set time" (the order of revelation), had come, the will of man could put off the event for thousands of years, what certainty is there in any promise or prophecy?

God has given His people, through Moses, a test whereby a true prophet should be known, saying: "If the thing follow not, nor come to pass, that is the thing which the Lord hath not spoken, but the prophet hath spoken it presumptuously" (Deut. 18:22). According to this test, what do those who hold the postponement theory make of the Lord's prophecy "the kingdom of God is at hand," when they say that the kingdom of which the Lord spoke was postponed because of its (supposed) rejection by the Jews?

Finally we come to the assertion (which is at the very foundation of the postponement theory), that "the Davidic Kingdom," meaning thereby the earthly Kingdom the Jews were expecting, was the next thing in order at the time of the Lord's first coming. This statement we wish to bring in the most definite way to the test of Scripture.

It would be, of course, a task of great magnitude to review the Old Testament prophecies and show the various subjects they embrace, and their sequence--where any sequence can be discerned. But our object can be accomplished without any such laborious undertaking. For we have in the New Testament certain inspired summaries of the prophecies, by which the editor's statement can be tested. To these we will make our appeal.

For example, in 1 Peter 1:10-12 we have a general summing up of what the prophets foretold; and this will answer perfectly our purpose. [2]

In the first place, the subject of the prophecies is divided by the apostle Peter into two great parts, (1) "the sufferings of the Christ," and (2) "the glories that should follow." So we have here not only the grand subject of the prophecies, in its two divisions, but we have "the order of revelation as it then stood"; for we are told precisely that "the glories" (plural in the original) were to follow the sufferings. Inasmuch then as the Throne is the prominent feature of "the glories" of the Christ, it is clear that the Throne was not "the next thing in order."

But that is not all. For the Scripture last cited tells us plainly that the theme of the prophets was--not the earthly kingdom, which is not referred to or hinted at in this summary, but--the "salvation" and the "Grace" which were to come unto us. This is an exceedingly important statement, and when its meaning (which is transparently plain) is grasped, it is seen to be conclusive of the question we are now examining.

And not only so, but it was revealed to those prophets that the things they foretold were ministered "not unto themselves, but unto us"; and the passage tells further that the very same things which the prophets foretold are what "are now reported unto you by them that have preached the gospel unto you with the Holy Ghost sent down .from heaven."

Thus we have it here declared in the plainest words that the general theme of the prophets is the same as that of the preachers of the gospel; that what the prophets of old predicted is exactly what the evangelists now preach! Thus we learn that the "gospel"--that is to say God's message of grace for all the world--was the prominent subject of the Old Testament prophecy, and was "next in order" to "follow" the sufferings of Christ, which were immediately due for fulfilment when He came into the world. Again, in addressing the company of Gentiles assembled in the home of Cornelius, the apostle gives a concise summary of the message which God had sent unto the children of Israel, "which was published throughout all Judea, and began from Galilee after the baptism which John preached" (cf. Mark 1:4-14) and that message (or "word") consisted--not in preaching the earthly kingdom, but in "preaching peace through Jesus Christ" (Acts 10:36, 37).

The testimony of Paul agrees perfectly with this. His preaching and writing were based firmly upon the prophets: and when he speaks of what was "promised afore," it is not the earthly kingdom, but "the gospel of God concerning His Son." This, says the apostle, is what "He had promised afore by His prophets in the Holy Scriptures" (Rom. 1:1-3). Moreover, the theme of the Epistle to the Romans is the righteousness of God in justifying believing sinners; and this (not the earthly kingdom at all) is what the apostle says expressly was "witnessed by the law and the prophets" (Rom. 3:21). Paul also in his defense of his ministry before Herod Agrippa testified that, from the beginning of his commission as a servant of Christ unto that very day, he had continued "witnessing both to small and great, saying none other things than those which the prophets and Moses did say should come" (Acts 26:22). This is another positive assertion that the evangelists now preach exactly what the prophets foretold.

The witness of "all the prophets" is also stated by Peter in, the house of Cornelius in a very familiar verse: "To Him (Christ) give all the prophets witness, that through His Name, whosoever believeth in Him shall receive remission of sins" (Acts 10:43).

The words of Zacharias, spoken before the Lord was born, are likewise very clear, and are decisive of the matter in dispute. The whole prophecy (Luke 1:67-79) should be read attentively; but for our immediate purpose it is enough to quote the opening words, which tell clearly what the new dispensation was to be--namely one of Redemption and

Salvation--and tell also what it was that God had spoken by the mouth of His holy prophets "since the world began," that is, from a time long before there was any earthly nation of Israel:

"Blessed be the Lord God of Israel; for He hath visited and redeemed His people, and hath raised up an horn of Salvation for us in the house of His servant David; as He spake by the mouth of His holy prophets which have been since the world began."

See also the concluding verses (77-79) which tell specifically what the coming "Salvation" was--"the remission of sins," "light" to them in darkness and the shadow of death, and a "way of peace."

Other New Testament summaries of the prophecies might be referred to, but we will only cite in conclusion the Lord's own words recorded in the last chapter of Luke. There we find His explanations to the two disciples with whom He walked and talked by the way, and whom He reproved for not believing "all that the prophets have spoken" (ver. 25). The words which follow make it clear that the theme of the prophets was, just as we saw from 1 Peter, "the sufferings of Christ and the glory that should follow." For the Lord said: "Ought not Christ to have suffered these things, and to enter into His glory?" And that such was necessary He proceeded to prove. For "Beginning at Moses and all the prophets, He expounded unto them in all the Scriptures, the things concerning Himself." Clearly then, the two great divisions of the prophetic Scriptures were Christ's sufferings and death on earth, and His glory as a Man in Heaven. (See John 12:23; 13:32; 17:5; Acts 2:33; 4:13; 1 Tim. 3:16; Heb. 2:9 etc.). In other words, the main theme of the prophets, when spiritually discerned is that which is fulfilled and being fulfilled through Jesus Christ, during this present age.

The same order of fulfilment of prophecy appears in the words of the Lord recorded in the last part of the same chapter (Luke 24:44-49), that order being, first His own sufferings, then His resurrection and the glory into which He was about to enter in heaven, and then the coming of the Holy Ghost and the preaching of the gospel among all nations. We quote the words, which are so clear as to need no comment:

"And He said unto them, These are the words which I spake unto you while I was yet with you, that all things must be fulfilled, which were written in the law of Moses, and in the prophets, and in the psalms concerning Me. Then opened He their understanding that they might understand the Scriptures, and said unto them, Thus it is written, and thus it behooved (i.e. was necessary for) Christ to suffer and to rise from the dead the third day; and that repentance and remission of sins should be preached in His Name among all nations beginning at Jerusalem. And ye are witnesses of these things. And behold, I send the promise of My

Father upon you: but tarry ye in the city of Jerusalem, until ye be endued with power from on high."

In these words we have the Lord's own explanation of "the order of revelation as it then stood" (and as of course it has always stood) : and we see that, in the progress of those great events as declared by Him Who is both the Subject and the Fulfiller of all the prophecies, the earthly kingdom had no place at all among the purposes He had come to accomplish.

Notes

1. In the original Greek there is strong emphasis upon the word "is," which emphasis does not appear in our versions.
2. The passage reads in part: "Receiving the end of your faith, the salvation of your souls, of which salvation the prophets have inquired who prophesied of the grace which should come unto you: searching what, or what manner of time the Spirit of Christ Who was in them did signify when He testified beforehand the sufferings of Christ, and the glories that should follow."

Chapter Eight - The Kingdom Foretold By The Prophets

THE teaching of dispensationalism concerning the Kingdom is apparently founded upon two mistaken ideas; first, that the Kingdom foretold by the prophets of old--especially when the prophecy related to David or his house--was the earthly kingdom of Israel; second, that "the next thing in order" on the Divine program was the national restoration and earthly supremacy for the Jews. These two suppositions being taken for granted, it is easy to assume further that the Kingdom which the Lord said was at hand was the earthly kingdom.

But in fact both the ideas set forth above are erroneous; for the Scriptures clearly prove that the Kingdom foretold by the prophets was the very same Kingdom of God based upon the death and resurrection of the Son of David, which was brought into the world by the coming of the Holy Spirit, and which has been extended throughout all the nations of earth, and through all the centuries of this era of grace "by those who have preached the gospel with the Holy Ghost sent down from heaven."

And in particular we are able to show that the prophecies which refer to David and his Seed have their fulfilment during this present age. The main facts concerning the Davidic prophecies are:

1.   The work which, according to those prophecies, the promised Son of David was to accomplish was the two-fold work of saving sinners from

among all nations and building the House of God (the church). Both parts of this two-fold work are presented in the Gospel of Matthew.

2.   The "throne" covenanted to David's Son was the throne of the universe, not the throne of the earthly Israel.

3.   The prophecies require for their fulfilment that the promised Son of David should first suffer and die before He could reign, whether in heaven or on earth.

This third point is of special value for our present purposes, in that it makes it quite impossible that the earthly kingdom, even if such a thing were foretold at all, could have been proclaimed, or even contemplated, in the days of the Lord's earthly ministry. It makes certain that the only kingdom which was, or could have been in view, was the spiritual Kingdom of God which was to be founded upon the death and resurrection of the "Son," the "Christ" of God, Who also was God's "King," spoken of by David in the Second Psalm.

The fact that the expected Son of David must needs have suffered and risen again ere He could reign (whether in heaven or on earth), is clearly set forth by the apostle Peter in Acts 2:25-31; where he quotes Psalm 16 and explains that David was not speaking of himself when he said "Thou wilt not leave my soul in hell, neither wilt Thou suffer Thine Holy One to see corruption," but was speaking of Christ. And then he further explains that David "being a prophet, and knowing that God had sworn with an oath to him, that of the fruit of his loins, according to the flesh, He would raise up Christ to sit on his throne; he seeing this before, spake of the resurrection of Christ."

This gives us plainly the true meaning of God's word and His oath to David in regard to the Throne, showing that the promise was to be fulfilled in resurrection.

Clearly then the Davidic promise would lead us to expect, not an earthly kingdom at Christ's coming, but just what happened, namely His death, resurrection and ascension and His enthronement in heaven at God's right hand, as foretold in Psalm 110, which Peter proceeds immediately to quote and apply (v. 33).

It is appropriate at this point to remind the reader that the Kingdom of Israel is not the Kingdom of God and was never called by that name. Therefore the very terms of the announcement made by Christ and His forerunner are proof to all who know the Scriptures that, whatever it was that God was then about to do, it was not the restoration of the earthly glories of Israel's vanished sovereignty.

And specially is it to be remembered that the true Israel was never at anytime, in the purpose of God, an earthly nation or Kingdom. This being recognized, it will be clearly perceived without any further help from the

Scriptures, that the whole rabbinical doctrine of an earthly Kingdom over which the Messiah, the son of David was to reign and to which all the nations of the world were to be tributory, was from top to bottom a work of their carnal imagination.

Turning back to Numbers 23:9 we read the word which Jehovah put in Balaam's mouth, that "the people (of Israel) shall dwell alone, and shall not be reckoned among the nations." And Moses, speaking to God, had said: "So shall we be separated, I and Thy people, from all the people that are upon the face of the earth" (Ex. 33:16). For God's purpose was that Israel should "dwell in safety alone" (Deut. 33:28). And that is still His will for those who are in His Kingdom (2 Cor. 6:17; Phil. 3:20).

Therefore, pursuant to this purpose, the Lord Himself became their King, and reigned over them, until, as a punishment for their rebellion against Him, He gave them their own desire and made them into an earthly kingdom, with a human king, "like all the nations." The record of this transcendently important event is in I Samuel, Chapter 8. There we read (v. 4) that: "All the elders of Israel gathered themselves together and came to Samuel unto Ramah, and said unto him, Behold, thou art old, and thy sons walk not in thy ways; now make us a king to judge us like all the nations."

This action of the nation by its elders displeased Samuel; but the Lord instructed him to hearken to the voice of the people, and to grant them their petition, in all they had asked; because,--and let the reason be noted and weighed - "They have not rejected thee, but they have rejected Me, THAT I SHOULD NOT REIGN OVER THEM" (v. 7).

Thus Israel formally rejected the Lord as their King; and this, as He proceeds in the succeeding verses to declare, was the culmination of all their unfaithfulness and apostasy from the day He had brought them up out of Egypt even unto that day.

The earthly Kingdom of Israel, therefore, was the expression of God's high displeasure with that people. As He said to them long afterward, [1] "gave thee a king in Mine anger" (Hos. 13:11). And yet this is the Kingdom for whose restoration the rabbis of old were fatuously looking; and which they were so confidently expecting that they made it the foundation of their whole system of doctrine. Is there then anything stranger among the religious vagaries of our times than that the very same fatuous notion should have become the foundation of a strictly novel system of Christian doctrine? And does it not heighten the wonder that the leading teachers of that new system, with its foundation of sand, should be prominent amongst those who have elected to call themselves, Fundamentalists?

It was, of course, to be expected that the Jews of Christ's day should have seen in the prophecies only what they wished to see--that is to say, the era of Israel's earthly greatness. It is quite natural that they should have construed the prophecies in accordance with their own carnal desires and thoughts. And we have it on the highest authority that it was because they knew not their expected Messiah, when He came to them, "nor yet the voices of the prophets which are read every Sabbath day, that they have fulfilled them in condemning Him" (Acts 13:27). Therefore it is not surprising that the coming of Christ should have meant for them nothing more or other than political deliverance from their Roman oppressors. But it is a cause for surprise, and for deep sorrow as well, that learned commentators in our day, men whose views are widely accepted as authoritative, should make the same fatal mistake. And the marvel of it is the greater because the New Testament Scriptures have made it plain to all Christians that the Kingdom foretold by the prophets of Israel and announced by Christ and His servants, is of a spiritual character--"not eating and drinking," as the earthly minded Jews supposed (and still do), "but righteousness, and peace and joy, in the Holy Ghost" (Rom. 14:17).

The two disciples with whom the Lord walked on the way to Emmaus (Luke 24:13-27), and who were disappointed and grieved because they had hoped that it had been He who should have redeemed Israel, were rebuked by Him as "Fools (or senseless ones) and slow of heart to believe all that the prophets have spoken." And thereupon, "beginning at Moses and all the PROPHETS" He proceeded to show them that the entire prophetic word made it necessary that He Who was "the Christ" should suffer those very things and enter into His glory.

Very likely we have felt pity for those foolish disciples, who ignorantly cherished an idea so contrary to the purposes of God as revealed by all His holy prophets since the world began. Yet surely much allowance is to be made for them, seeing that they were Israelites in the flesh, that they were actually under the heel of a despotic heathen power; and especially, seeing that their accredited teachers unanimously construed the prophecies in that sense. But how can we account for the fact that, in spite of the expositions of prophecy by the Lord Himself and by His inspired apostles which dispel completely the thought that the Lord's first coming had anything whatever to do with the national independence of Israel, learned men of our day have revived that exceedingly "Jewish" idea, and have made it the corner stone of their system of teaching? A discerning servant of Christ has lately said that we have here the most extraordinary phenomenon to be found within the pale of orthodox Christianity.

In the present chapter I propose to examine some of the prophecies which refer specifically to David, the object being to ascertain just what was promised in that connection. It is often taken for granted nowadays that, where David's name is mentioned in a prophecy, the subject thereof is the earthly greatness of the nation Israel. In fact that idea has so completely taken possession of the minds of certain teachers that the very mention of David's name in a passage of Scripture (as Matthew 1:1) is regarded as sufficient warrant for calling it "Jewish." But the truth of the matter is that the prophecies linked with the name and history of David have to do specially with the gospel, and with the House of God, that is to say the Church.

What those prophecies really called for was the coming, through David's line, of One Who should be the Saviour of the world. The gospel of God concerning His Son "which He had promised afore by His prophets" was connected with David as much as, and as closely as, with Abraham. Paul makes this very clear in the beginning of his inspired explanation of the gospel given in his Epistle to the Romans, where he says that "the gospel of God" was "concerning His Son" who was "of the seed of David according to the flesh" (Rom. 1:1-3). And the same apostle recalls this fundamental point of gospel-truth very emphatically in his last message in which he says: "Remember Jesus Christ of the seed of David raised from the dead according to my gospel" (2 Tim. 2:8, R.V.).

It is greatly to be regretted that David's connection with the gospel has been almost wholly lost sight of in our day; for the facts in that regard are necessary to an understanding of the breadth and fulness of the gospel-message. However, it is not a difficult matter for any who are interested to possess themselves of those facts. We have endeavored to set them forth in some detail in a work entitled "Bringing Back the King," in the section entitled "The Sure Mercies of David." Hence we will confine ourselves at present to the consideration of only a few prominent points.

The main fact to be grasped is that the special promises of God which He is fulfilling in our day of grace and salvation, were given and covenanted to the two men, Abraham and David. Thus the gospel rests upon these two pedestals; and the promises to David (or concerning David's Seed) were just as much for all mankind as were the promises to Abraham and his "SEED." God made His "everlasting covenant" with Abraham (Gen. 17-7), and also with David (2 Sam. 23:5). It was the same covenant; and it was to be established by the death and resurrection of the promised "Seed"; for we read in Hebrews 13:20 of "the blood of the everlasting covenant," which was shed by Jesus Christ. Moreover, our Lord Himself, in instituting His memorial Supper, said of the cup, "This cup is the new covenant in My blood which is shed for you" (Lu. 22:20).

We might concisely summarize the Gospel of God's grace as that Divine message which brings to sinners of all nations "The blessing of Abraham" and "The sure mercies of David"; and since the "blessing" and the "mercies" are all secured through Jesus Christ, it is evident that Matthew 1:1 is the opening of this era of grace.

The "everlasting covenant" which God made with those two men was an unconditional covenant, that is to say a covenant of grace. Since God alone was bound by it, there could be no failure in it. That covenant had to do with matters which are infinitely great and of everlasting duration, namely, the Family, the Inheritance, the Blessing, (i.e. the Holy Spirit, Gal. 3:14), the Throne, and the House. Of these five infinitely great things the first three were embraced in God's promises to Abraham, and the last two in His promises to David.1 With these simple facts in mind we will be able to arrive at a clear understanding of the main features of the Davidic prophecies.

All the five great things mentioned above are embraced in the "Salvation of God," which is now proclaimed by the Gospel to sinners of all nations, in the Name of "Jesus Christ of the Seed of David raised from the dead." All of them depend absolutely upon the blood of Jesus Christ the Lamb of God, apart from which there could have been no blessing of any sort whether for Jew or Gentile. Apart from the blood of atonement there was nothing for mankind but condemnation; for at the time of Christ's first coming "all the world" had become "guilty before God." It is simply an impossibility that an earthly kingdom could have been announced by God's servants at that time, if ever.

God's gospel is, as we have seen, that "which He had promised afore by His PROPHETS"; and therefore we must turn back to the prophets to find out just what the gospel-promises were and are. It is a greatly impoverished gospel when the promises concerning David's Seed are taken from it, are characterized as "Jewish," and are "postponed" to another age than this, and to another people than the redeemed of this age. And that is exactly what is being done under our very eyes. Let us therefore awake out of sleep, and realize what is going on.

Paul puts the matter very clearly also in his words recorded in Acts 13:22, 23, where, speaking in a Jewish synagogue concerning the people of Israel, he recalled that God, after removing Saul from the throne, had "raised up unto them David to be their king"; and he said: "Of this man's seed hath God, according to His promise, raised unto Israel a Saviour, Jesus." It was therefore, a Saviour that God had promised to Israel through David's line; for it was a Saviour that Israel needed as much as other peoples of the world. The restoration of the earthly kingdom would not have met their need; much less would it have met the need of the world. That, however, was not in view at all. For "when the fulness of the time was come" and "God sent forth His Son" it was "to redeem them that were under the law" (Gal. 4:4, 5), not to restore their earthly greatness. And likewise, when Christ Jesus proclaimed with His own lips, "The time is fulfilled, Repent ye and believe the gospel" (Mk. 1:15), it was of "the Kingdom of God" He was speaking, and not of the earthly kingdom and He called it "the gospel."

The apostle Paul in the discourse from which we have just quoted showed that the "Saviour" Whom God had raised up to Israel from the Seed of David was not for Israel only, but for "all who believe in Him"; and this is in exact agreement with the proclamation made by the angel of the Lord to the shepherds who were watching their flocks by night at the time of the Lord's birth. The angel's words were "Fear not: for behold I bring you good tidings of great joy which shall be to all people. For unto you is born this day in the city of David a Saviour, which is Christ the Lord."

It is strange that this proclamation from heaven, which gives the Lord's full designation "Christ the Lord," and His birth "in the city of David," and the purpose of His coming, as "Saviour" for "all people," has been so completely ignored in the discussion of the matter in hand; for its decisive bearing thereon is evident. Much is made of the fact that the heathen Magi, who saw the star in the East, came with the query: "Where is he that is born King of the Jews?" (Mat. 2:2). That question of the Magi is often referred to as if it proved that Christ had come in connection with the earthly kingdom. It ought not to be necessary to say that the question asked by those Magi proves nothing of the sort. Coming from the East where the memory of Daniel's and Ezekiel's prophecies was doubtless preserved, and possibly Balaam's also (Num. 24:17), they probably had received light in regard thereto. Moreover, the Lord was and is "the King of the Jews"; so that the question of the Magi was an intelligent one. It does not indicate at all that they were expecting the national emancipation of the Jews; for that would have had no special interest for them. The more reasonable explanation of their interest in the birth of Christ, and of the trouble they took to pay homage and "offer gifts" to Him (Psa. 72:10), was that it had been in some way revealed to them that the One who was born "King of the Jews" was to bring blessing also to the Gentiles. Therefore the coming of the Magi "to worship" Christ indicates an event of far greater importance than the birth of an heir to the throne of David. It is recorded that the Magi were "warned of God in a dream that they should not return to Herod," from which it appears that they were being divinely guided in their mission.

It is clear, therefore, that the bearing of this incident is not at all what the advocates of the postponement theory make of it.

But the message of the angel to the shepherds at Bethlehem was an authoritative announcement direct from heaven; and it was given in plain words that leave nothing to conjecture. It tells the precise purpose for which Christ had been born; and its terms shut out all possibility that an earthly kingdom was in view. Indeed the purpose for which God sent forth His Son has been repeatedly declared in messages straight from heaven, through angels and men, as Zacharias and Simeon, and later by the inspired apostles, as well as by the Lord Himself. In not one of these declarations concerning the object of His coming is there the slightest hint of an earthly kingdom; but on the contrary they one and all reveal purposes utterly inconsistent with it. Nevertheless, in the interest of dispensationalism all these clear declarations are swept aside, while other passages of Scripture are forced and wrested in order to make them yield to it a semblance of support.

It is a significant fact that while the message brought by the angel Gabriel to Zacharias, who was to be the father of the Lord's forerunner, was the first communication from heaven to earth after the stream of Old Testament prophecy had ended in Malachi, the first human lips that were opened to prophesy the beginning of the new and long awaited era of blessing were those of the women Elizabeth and Mary (Luke 1:41-55). The words uttered by the latter tell clearly that the new era then about to begin was to be--not that of any earthly kingdom whatever, but--that of "the mercy" promised to the fathers, "to Abraham and his seed forever." And it was subsequently revealed through Paul that the "seed of Abraham" who were to inherit the promises are those who believe the gospel. For we read: "Know ye, therefore, that they which are of faith, the same are the children of Abraham" (Gal. 3:7). And again: "For ye are all the children of God by faith in Jesus Christ... And if ye be Christ's, then are ye Abraham's seed, and heirs according to the promise" (Id. 3:26, 29).

In view, therefore of what has been said above I may briefly summarize the various predictions concerning the Seed of David by saying that what God promised to give through David's line was not an earthly King for the Jews, but a Saviour for all the world.

Matthew records in his first chapter that He Who was born of the virgin of David's line was a Saviour, and was named "Jehovah-Saviour" before His birth (Matt. 1:21). Zacharias, the father of John the Baptist, prophesied of the Coming One as being a Saviour, saying that God had raised up an horn of Salvation in the house of His servant David; and further said that this raising up a Saviour in the house of David was in fulfilment of what God had spoken "by the mouth of His holy prophets...since the world began" (Lu. 1:68-70). Thus we learn (and many other Scriptures declare the same fact) that what was required for the fulfilment of that which all the prophets foretold was the coming in the house of David--not of an earthly king, but of--a Saviour.

Zacharias further prophesied concerning the ministry of John the Baptist that he was to go before the face of the Lord to prepare His ways-- not to give notice of an earthly kingdom but--"to give knowledge of salvation unto His people by the remission of their sins" (Lu. 1:77).

The angel of the Lord, in announcing the birth of Jesus to the shepherds on Bethlehem's plain, spake not a word of His having come to reign over Israel, but proclaimed good tidings of great joy for all people; saying: "For unto you is born this day in the city of David a Saviour which is Christ, the Lord" (Lu. 2:10, 11). Here again, in a message brought straight from heaven, the promised One of David's line is announced as a Saviour for all men, not a King for the Jews.

Simeon also, being filled with the Holy Ghost, and led by the Holy Ghost to the temple, took the infant Son of David from His virgin mother's arms and spake of Him as God's "Salvation" which He had "prepared before the face of all people"; and as "a Light to lighten the Gentiles" (Lu. 2:30-32). Thus the inspired messages through men and angels all testify clearly that the One Who had come of David's

line was the Saviour and Light of the world.

In due time "the word of God came to John the son of Zacharias in the wilderness," and he preached to all the people of Israel. His message was in perfect accord with the word of all the PROPHETS; for he announced the coming of a Saviour Who should give His life for all men--"the Lamb of God which taketh away the sin of the world"--and declared that "all flesh" (Jew and Gentile) should "see the Salvation of God" (John 1:29; Lu. 3:6).

We have also the testimony of the Lord Himself, the true and faithful Witness, declaring that He came not to be ministered unto" (that is to be served as kings are served) "but to minister, and to give His life a ransom for many" (Matt. 20:28). We have this same testimony from His own lips in many other passages (as Luke 4:18-21). And we have also the "good confession" which He witnessed before Pontius Pilate when falsely accused before him of attempting to set up an earthly throne, saying: "My Kingdom is not of this world" (John 18:36; cf. Luke 4:5).

The apostles likewise, after the death and resurrection of Christ and their baptism with the Holy Ghost as promised by John the Baptist, proclaimed the same tidings of a Saviour for all men, Who had been raised up in the house of David. Thus Peter preached concerning David that he "being a prophet, and knowing that God had sworn with an oath to him that of the fruit of his loins, according to the flesh, He would raise up Christ to sit on His throne; he (David) seeing this before spake of the resurrection of Christ"; and Peter continues the explanation of the prophecies concerning Christ, making it clear that the throne which He was to occupy in resurrection, according to God's oath to David, was the throne of God in heaven (Acts 2:29-36).

And again Peter preached concerning Christ, saying: "Him hath God exalted with His right hand to be a Prince and a Saviour, for to give repentance to Israel, and forgiveness of sins" (Acts 5:31).

Paul also connects God's salvation for all men with David, saying, "Of this man's seed hath God, according to His promise, raised unto Israel a Saviour" (Acts 13:22, 23). And in his epistle to the Romans, the same apostle unfolds "the gospel of God; which He had promised afore by His prophets in the Holy Scriptures," telling us that the promised gospel of God was "concerning His Son, which was made of the seed of David, according to the flesh" (Rom. 1:1-3). And the last words of this great preacher and apostle of the Gentiles in regard to the gospel proclaimed by himself, is a stirring exhortation to "Remember Jesus Christ of the seed of David, raised from the dead according to my gospel" (2 Tim. 2:8, R.V.).

Thus we have the concurrent testimony of PROPHETS, angels, Spirit-filled men (Zacharias and Simeon), the Lord's forerunner who also was filled with the Holy Ghost from his mother's womb (Lu. 1:15), of the Lord Jesus Himself, and of the inspired apostles,--all declaring with one voice that God's promise and purpose from of old, was to raise up of the seed of David One Who should save His people by the sacrifice of Himself, and should be straightway exalted to the heavenly throne of a heavenly kingdom. The whole voice of Scripture,--both in the Law, the PROPHETS, the Psalms, the Gospels, the preaching of the apostles in the book of Acts, and their teaching in the Epistles,--tells the same clear story of the steadfast purpose of God. In the light of these Scriptures, and of many others of like nature, it is as clear as that divine light can make it, that the Kingdom, promised afore by the prophets to the Son of David, was and is that spiritual and heavenly Kingdom which that promised Son of David first announced, and then introduced by His death and resurrection, by sending down the Holy Ghost after He had been exalted to the throne of the Majesty in the heavens, and by sending forth the gospel into all the world.

Note

1. See "Our Liberty in Christ: A Study in Galatians" by P. Mauro, chapter on 'The Everlasting Covenant."

Chapter Nine - The Kingdom Foretold by the Prophets (Cont.)

In the "Reference Bible" whose teachings we are examining the following is from a note on Matthew 3:2--

"The phrase 'Kingdom of heaven' signifies the Messianic earth rule of Jesus Christ, the Son of David." "It is the Kingdom covenanted to David's seed, described in the PROPHETS."

I have two brief comments to make upon this dogmatic statement; first, that not a scrap of evidence is offered in support of it, and second that it is in flat contradiction to the great cloud of witnesses whose unanimous testimony I have cited above.

Then follows a note on the same chapter in which it is stated that "The Kingdom of heaven" has three aspects in Matthew, of which the second aspect (b) is in seven 'mysteries of the Kingdom of heaven' to be fulfilled during the present age," etc.

This statement as to there being "three aspects" of the one Kingdom; one of these "aspects" being "in seven mysteries...to be fulfilled in this age," is very confusing. So far as I can see, it is not only without the slightest support in the Scriptures, but is altogether unintelligible.

Let it be noted, however, that we have here a clear admission that the Kingdom of heaven does exist during the present age. It matters not what is meant by the Kingdom's existing now in one "aspect" and now in another. It does exist now. Our Lord's prophetic parables in Matthew XIII, in which He foretold what the Kingdom of heaven which He had announced as at hand, was to be "like," were too much for the editor's theory. For no one can close his eyes to the fact that those parables marvelously describe God's work and His spiritual Kingdom during this present age. Very well then, how does the case stand upon this admission? Our Lord said the Kingdom of heaven was at hand, and He told what it would be like; and the event showed (as the editor here admits) that it was at hand, and that its likeness is precisely what the Lord said it would be. If so, what becomes of the basic doctrine of dispensationalism that the Kingdom of heaven our Lord announced as at hand was withdrawn and postponed? Manifestly, the editor's admission destroys that notion completely.

The case is very strong; and to realize this we have only to remember that in the days of Christ the Jews were occupying their own land and were enjoying a sort of national existence and a measure of independence. Yet at that time "the Kingdom of heaven" (whatever it was) had not yet come. Neither was the earthly kingdom then in existence; nor has it come, up to the present time. But "the Kingdom of heaven" did come immediately, even as Christ said it would come; and moreover, it took precisely the form and "likeness" predicted by the Lord in His parables. This the editor finds it necessary to admit. But how about the national existence of Israel, which the editor says is "the Kingdom of heaven?" What happened to that? So far from anything coming to pass in the nature of an earthly kingdom as expected by the Jews, what actually happened was the complete destruction of their city, temple, and nation, and the scattering of the people throughout the world, even to this very day. In a word, every vestige of their national existence was forthwith blotted out.

It is clear, therefore, that the "Kingdom of heaven," which formed the subject of the Lord's preaching and teaching, and the earthly kingdom for which the Jews were and still are looking, are not one and the same, but are distinct and utterly different the one from the other.

Turning back now to some of the principal prophecies concerning David, we shall find that while the prophets did not describe "the Kingdom of God" by name, they did describe the main features of this era of world-wide blessing to which the name "Kingdom of God" is given in the New Testament.

We may appropriately begin with the great prophecy found in Isaiah chapters 7-12. The words "and there shall come forth a Rod out of the stem of Jesse, and a Branch shall grow out of his roots" definitely connect this prophecy with the House of David. (See also Isa. 7:13, 14). We give it the first place in our examination because it is the first prophecy quoted in the New Testament. It is therefore a very significant Scripture, both as determining the nature of the era which began when Christ was born of a virgin of the house and lineage of David; and also as fixing the character of Matthew's Gospel. For in the first chapter of Matthew we have the angel's message concerning the Virgin Mary, in which he said:

"And she shall bring forth a son, and thou shalt call His Name Jesus: for He shall save His people from their sins. Now all this was done that it might be fulfilled which was spoken of the Lord by the prophet, saying, Behold the [1] virgin shall be with child, and shall bring forth a Son, and they shall call His Name Emmanuel, which being interpreted is God with us."

We have here the first statement in New Testament Scriptures of the purpose for which the Lord the Son of David was coming into the world. It tells of One about to be born in David's line Who should "save His people from their sins"--in other words of the birth of a Saviour. Moreover, and this is the point we wish to emphasize, it plainly declares that the birth of the One Who was to save His people from their sins was the fulfilment of the prophecy of Isaiah 7:14. Hence there is no room for any uncertainty as to the meaning of that prophecy. It foretold an era of salvation for sinners, not of earthly greatness for Israel. It foretold the coming of the Lord for the express purpose of doing a work whereby His people were to be saved from their sins. It is therefore a prophecy of the cross, not of an earthly throne. This is what we find at the very beginning of Matthew's Gospel (which is commonly disparaged as "Jewish"), and in connection with the House of David.

With this clear light it is easy to see many details in Isaiah's prophecy-- especially in chapters 11 and 12--which are fulfilled in this present age. Verse 10 of chapter 11 is specially significant:

"And in that day there shall be a Root of Jesse which shall stand for an ensign of the people: to it (or to Him) shall the Gentiles seek, and His rest shall be glory." (Margin.)

Here is a distinct promise of salvation for "Gentiles" through this "Root of Jesse." And not only so, but this very verse is quoted by Paul in Romans 15:12, who thus definitely links his gospel with that announced in the first chapter of Matthew. The way the verse is quoted by Paul, and the meaning thereby assigned to it by the Holy Spirit, is remarkable and illuminating. This is the quotation:

"And again Esaias saith, There shall be a Root of Jesse, and He that shall rise to reign over the Gentiles,' in Him shall the Gentiles trust."

Here is a Kingdom-promise indeed. It tells of One Who should "rise to reign." But the Kingdom here foretold is the very opposite of the Kingdom expected by the Jews; for the passage, as thus divinely interpreted, had reference to One Who was to "reign over the Gentiles," and in Whom the Gentiles should trust (or have hope).

This portion of Isaiah is again quoted by Matthew at chapter 4:14-16, the quotation being from Isaiah 9:1, 2. There we find the foretelling of Christ's ministry, which was to begin in "Galilee of the Gentiles" (a very significant statement); and also of the nature of His ministry, which was to be the giving of light (and by implication life also) to them that "sat in darkness" and in "the region and shadow of death." These are words of the clearest gospel-significance, words which are so well understood that we need not dwell upon them. It surely goes a long way toward settling the disputed question of the character of Matthew's Gospel, that the prophecies cited at the very beginning of that Gospel, and declared to have been "fulfilled"--the one at the birth of Christ and the other at the commencement of His ministry--have nothing whatever to do with an earthly kingdom and everything to do with salvation for the whole world.

But we have also, in the passage last quoted (Mat. 4:14-16), a bit of evidence of the most definite and conclusive character as to the precise nature of the "Kingdom" which the Lord was then announcing as "at hand." For in what way and in what sense did the Lord "fulfil" the promise of bringing light and life to "Galilee of the Gentiles"? Verse 17 tells us plainly that He fulfilled it by proclaiming the message: "Repent ye, for the Kingdom of heaven is at hand." That message therefore had no reference at all to the earthly kingdom; for the Holy Spirit here testifies that it announced the era of promised blessing to the Gentiles. Thus it clearly appears that the prophecy of light to the Gentiles is fulfilled in the Kingdom of heaven.

PSALM 2

Another surpassingly important prophecy connected with David is the Second Psalm (a Psalm of David). This great prophecy is distinguished by the fact that it speaks of God's Christ ("My Anointed"), of God's Son, and of God's King. It would require a volume to point out in detail the bearings of this Psalm. But for present purposes we need not dwell long upon it. To begin with, the subject of an earthly kingdom is conspicuous only by its absence. The first part (the opposition of earth's rulers and peoples) was fulfilled in the crucifixion of Christ (Acts 4:25-28). The words "Thou art My Son" were spoken by the Father at the Lord's baptism, where His death and resurrection were figured, and where He received the anointing of the Holy Spirit for His ministry. Moreover, Paul explains that God fulfilled His promise to the fathers, "in that He bath raised up Jesus again; as it is also written in the Second Psalm, Thou art My Son; this day have I begotten Thee." This shows that the Second Psalm was a prophecy to be fulfilled in the resurrection of Christ. Furthermore, we have in the last verse of the Psalm the unmistakable gospel-promise: "Blessed are all they that put their trust in Him."

PSALM 72

This is the prayer of David the son of Jesse. It contains distinct promises concerning the Kingdom of David's promised Son. But it is plain that the prophecy has not to do with an earthly kingdom. For in verse 6 there is an evident reference to the first coming of Christ; for it speaks of the "rain" (the pouring out of the Holy Spirit) and the "showers" of blessing. The references to "righteousness and peace" in this part of the Psalm point to the Kingdom of God as it now is (Rom. 14:17). The words "And men shall be blessed in Him; all nations shall call Him blessed" (v. 17), point also to this present era, during which the gospel is being preached to all nations in obedience to Matthew 28:19 while verses 8-11 declaring the extent of His dominion "to the ends of the earth," indicate the universal Kingdom of glory that is yet to come.

This Psalm is specially pertinent in that it records the Lord's covenant and oath to David in these words:

"I have made a covenant with My chosen, I have sworn unto David My servant; Thy seed will I establish forever, and build up thy throne to all generations: Selah" (verses 3, 4).

"My covenant will I nor break, nor alter the thing that is gone out of My lips. Once have I sworn by My holiness that I will not lie unto David. His seed shall endure forever and his throne as the sun before Me" (verses 34-36).

The Psalm is written to celebrate "the Mercies of the Lord;" and its scope cannot be fully appreciated without a comprehension of what is meant by "the sure mercies of David," a subject too large to be entered upon now. It must suffice at this point to say that "the sure mercies of David" embrace the blessings of the gospel, and chiefly the forgiveness of sins. [2] But it is clear enough upon merely reading the Psalm that its subject is not the Jewish kingdom. Christ's "throne," which is prominently mentioned in it, is manifestly a throne of vastly greater dignity and glory than that of David or Solomon.

Moreover, we find in this prophetic Psalm references to various subjects not in any way connected with the earthly nation. It is promised that the heavens shall praise the wonders of the Lord (v. 5), suggesting the exaltation of the crucified and risen One to the highest heavens. The reference to "the congregation of the saints" (v. 5), and the statement "God is greatly to be feared in the assembly of saints," have an obvious application to this present age. It is, moreover, impossible to mistake the significance of these words:

"Mercy and truth shall go before Thy face. Blessed is the people that know the joyful sound, they shall walk, O Lord, in the light of Thy countenance. In Thy Name shall they rejoice all the day; and in Thy righteousness shall they be exalted" (v. 14-16).

Finally, verses 38-45 contain suggestions of the cutting off of David's line in the death of Christ. Verse 45 is very clear: "The days of His youth hast Thou shortened: Thou hast covered Him with shame, Selah." Then there are in verse 48 questions which are very significant in connection with the resurrection of Christ: "What man is he that liveth and shall not see death? Shall He deliver His soul from the hand of the grave? Selah."

This and other Scriptures, written of Christ as Son of David, indicate a fact which is made very clear in the gospel-preaching of both Peter and Paul, namely, that God's promises concerning the Son of David were to be fulfilled in resurrection. And this is the very essence of Paul's gospel, as appears by those remarkable words: "Remember Jesus Christ of the Seed of David raised from the dead according to my gospel" (2 Tim. 8, R.V.).

THE PROPHECIES OF JEREMIAH

The prophecies of Jeremiah are specially significant because spoken at the time when judgment was about to fall upon the people of Judah, and upon the occupants of the throne of David. We shall not attempt anything like an exposition of the many prophetic utterances from the lips of Jeremiah that have a bearing upon our subject. But we can, in a few words, call attention to certain things which fully bear out what we are seeking to show in this chapter.

In Jeremiah 23:5-8, we read:

"Behold the days come, saith the Lord, that I will raise unto David a righteous Branch, and a King shall reign and prosper, and shall execute judgment and justice in the earth."

This is doubtless one of the prophecies referred to by Peter in Acts 3:24; and we can see at a glance that the language strikingly corresponds with Peter's words in Acts 2:30, and Paul's in Acts 13:23, 33. Here we have a brief outline of "these days" of the Gospel, beginning with the coming of the "righteous Branch" of the house of David ("Jesus Christ the Righteous"). Manifestly this prophecy excludes the idea of an earthly kingdom during "the days" spoken of. It demands that the Righteous Branch of David should be a King and should reign and prosper, and should execute judgement and justice in the earth. In other words, it demands just what is fulfilled in the present Kingdom of heaven. The period to which the fulfilment of this prophecy belongs is definitely fixed by the title "THE LORD OUR RIGHTEOUSNESS"; for it is during this present era of grace that the Lord is specially revealed as the righteousness of His people. (1 Cor. 1:30; 2 Cor. 5:21; etc.)

The significance of this prophecy is intensified by that recorded in Chapter 33:15-26, beginning with the words:

"In those days and at that time will I cause the Branch of righteousness to grow up unto David; and He shall execute judgment and righteousness in the land (or earth)."

These words point clearly to the incarnation of the Lord, and to what was to follow. The "days" of which the prophet is here speaking were the days of "the new covenant" under which sins were to be forgiven and the laws of God were to be written in the hearts of His people. (Jer. 31:31-34). The period to which the fulfilment of this prophecy belongs is fixed in the most definite way by the words of the Lord in instituting His Supper, when He gave the cup to His disciples and said: "This is My blood of the new covenant which is shed for many for the remission of sins" (Mat.

26:28). The whole of chapters 31, 32, 33 of Jeremiah should be attentively read.

Coming now to the portion to which we are specially calling attention, we find in verses 17 and 18 (chap. 33) these promises:

"For thus saith the Lord, David shall never want a man" (or literally there shall not be cut off from David a man, see margin) "to sit upon the throne of the house of Israel; neither shall the priests the Levites want a man before Me to offer burnt offerings and to kindle meat offerings and to do sacrifice continually."

Obviously these wonderful promises are fulfilled in Jesus Christ, raised from the dead and glorified in heaven as a Priest after the order of Melchisedec, who was a king as well as a priest (Heb. 7:1, 2). After the Christ was "cut off" as foretold by Isaiah (53: 8) and Daniel (9:26), there was no man on earth to sit on David's throne; and after the destruction of Jerusalem (also foretold by Daniel 9:26) there were no priests on earth to offer the appointed sacrifices to God. But there is now and has been since the ascension of Christ, a Man in heaven to sit upon the throne of the house of Israel (the Israel of God). Moreover, God has also a Man before Him, as He said, to offer sacrifices continually (Heb. 8:3; 13:15).

It is easy, therefore, for us to see, in the light of the New Testament that Jeremiah's prophecy demanded that Christ should be born while the house of David still had a known existence in the world; and it demanded also the resurrection of Christ and His exaltation to heaven as both King and Priest. In other words, it demanded the very things which happened from and after the incarnation of Christ. So we have again a prophecy very definitely connected with David, and very definitely fulfilled in this gospel-era; a prophecy which excluded the possibility of an earthly kingdom's being announced at the Lord's first coming; if indeed such a thing were in God's contemplation at all.

THE PROPHECY OF ZECHARIAH

Finally, we refer to the remarkable and very precious prophecy concerning Christ (Zechariah 13:1-7), in which is found the oft-quoted reference to the wounds in His hands with which He was wounded in the house of His friends (v. 6). The chapter begins thus:

"In that day there shall be a fountain opened to the house of David for sin and for separation for uncleanness" (Margin).

Verse 7 indicates how the fountain was to be opened. For there we have the words: "Awake, O sword, against My Shepherd, and against the Man that is My Fellow. Smite the Shepherd, and the sheep shall be scattered." No doubt can exist as to the fulfilment of this prophecy, for the Lord Himself has applied it (Mat. 26:31; see also verse 54).

To get the full significance of this prophecy--one of the clearest of all the glorious gospel-prophecies--we must go back to the word of the Lord spoken to David by the prophet Nathan, whom God sent to bring home to David's conscience his awful sin in slaying his faithful servant Uriah, in order that he might take his wife. At that time Nathan said: "Now therefore the sword shall never depart from thine house." This must be kept in mind if we would understand David's connection with the gospel of God's grace. For we have two seemingly contradictory promises concerning David: first that God would build him a sure house and would "never" take away His mercies from him, and that he should "never" want a man to sit upon his throne; and second that the sword should "never" depart from his house. The latter promise was fulfilled when the sword of judgment was sheathed in the bosom of the Son of David; for by that stroke the house of David was "cut off," and cut off forever as an earthly thing. But the same stroke opened a fountain for sin and for uncleanness, wherein, by God's amazing grace, sinners of all nations may be cleansed from their sins. The other promises of this passage are, as we have already seen, fulfilled by Jesus Christ in resurrection.

In this connection we should recall Simeon's inspired words to Mary concerning "the sword" which was hanging over the house of David; for we remember that, after speaking of Christ as the "Light" that had come "to lighten the Gentiles" and to be the "glory of His people Israel," Simeon said to her: "Yea, a sword shall pierce through thine own soul also" (Lu. 2:35). This word spoken shortly after the birth of Christ is quite sufficient without any other Scripture, to prove that no earthly kingdom was in prospect at that time. But the proof is greatly strengthened by the fact that what Simeon's words indicated is just what was foretold by prophecies concerning the promised Son of David.

The concluding portion of Zechariah's prophecy foretells also the cutting off of the greater part of the inhabitants of the land, which occurred at the destruction of Jerusalem by Titus, A.D. 70; and the salvation of the remnant, of whom God said: "They shall I call upon My Name, and I will hear them: and I will say, It is My people; and they shall say, The Lord is my god" (Zech. 13:8, 9).

This passage does not deal with arithmetical "thirds." It does not foretell that a mathematical "third" of the Jewish nation would be saved, and the other two thirds be destroyed. What it indicates is that there would be three distinguishable groups or parties in the land. And so it was. For in Christ's day, as the Gospels make evident, there were (1) the scribes and Pharisees (2) the Sadducees, and (3) the publicans and sinners, It was the latter group which, as a class, listened to the message of Christ, and from which His disciples were drawn. Verse 9 is fulfilled in those who were saved through the Gospel. (Acts 2:21; Rom. 10:13; 1 Peter 2:9, 10.)

The promise of this prophecy of Zechariah of a fountain for sin and for uncleanness is seemingly very "Jewish," being limited to "the House of David." But the "mystery of the gospel" is this, that whereas all "the covenants and the promises" do indeed pertain to the Israelites (Rom. 9:4,5), God has, in His grace, made believing Gentiles to be "fellowheirs and partakers of His promise in Christ by (means of) the gospel" (Eph. 3:6). And especially does the gospel offer to all the world the unspeakable blessings of the "everlasting covenant, even the sure mercies of David" (Isa. 55:3). And moreover, it has now been revealed, as has been pointed out above, that the name "Jew" belongs properly to one who is a Jew inwardly, and "the Israel of God" embraces only the household of faith.

Notes

1. The definite article is in the original text.
2. See "Bringing Back the King," chapter on "The Sure Mercies of David."

Chapter Ten - The Law of Christ

THE character of every Kingdom is expressed in its law. Next in importance to the person of the king, and in what we call a "limited monarchy" or "constitutional Kingdom" above the king himself, is the law. In every case the keeping of the law involves first of all the honor of the king, and after that the peace of his realm and the welfare of his subjects. If therefore, the Kingdom of God have no law, it would not be a kingdom. Where then are we, whom God has translated into the kingdom of His dear Son, to look for the law of that Kingdom? No inquiry could be of greater importance for those who are saved by grace.

Every revelation of God's will for man is law; and His will is always "good and acceptable and perfect." "His commandments are not grievous." That is true always and everywhere. Man does not so regard it; but that is because man's state by nature, as a consequence of the fall of Adam, is a state of disobedience and lawlessness, and hence of enmity against God. "Because the mind of the flesh" (that which we all alike have by nature) "is enmity against God; for it is not subject to the law of God, neither indeed can be" (Rom. 8:7, marg).

Now the divine work of Redemption is, among other things, a process of recovering man from his natural state of lawlessness to a state of perfect submission to the will of God, which is a state of perfect happiness, unending bliss, joy unspeakable. It is a long process. In the course of its accomplishment God chose a particular people, all the off offspring of a man conspicuous for "the obedience of faith," which is gospel obedience (Rom. 1:5; 16:26), and He gave them His law in systematized form (a thing He had never done before, and has not done since; for "He hath not dealt so with any nation"). That gift of the law of God was a mark of special favor to that people; and the possession of it, notwithstanding their failure to keep it, or even to respect the Giver of it, has been nevertheless a source to them of unspeakable blessing.

This I feel constrained to insist upon and with all possible emphasis; for the reason that a special object of the dispensational teaching of the day apparently is to inspire in the people of God a feeling of aversion toward His law. Indeed the subject is sometimes presented in such a way as to give the impression that to be "under the law" is about the next thing to being in the lake of fire. [1]

One of the purposes of man's trial under the law was to make evident the hopeless corruption of his heart, and to convince him of the absolute necessity for a special work of God, whereby he might obtain the forgiveness of all his sins, and also gain a new life and nature. That is what Jesus Christ came to accomplish by His sacrificial death and by His resurrection from the dead; and that is why "the fulness of the time" for God to send forth His Son came not until after the trial of man under the law of Moses had made evident the necessity therefor.

Hence the trial of man under the law was by no means a failure. On the contrary, it accomplished just what God purposed thereby; and it was a most necessary stage of the long process of man's recovery from the dominion of sin. To be sure, it showed what a failure man himself is; and it made evident that because of the hopelessly corrupt state of his being he cannot obey a righteous and holy law, even though he recognizes it to be such (Rom. 7:12, 14, 15, 16), and even though he understands that his prosperity now and his welfare in eternity depend upon it. Those individuals who learned this while they were under the law, realized that they must cease from all self-efforts at salvation, and must cast themselves for that upon the mercy of God. All such, and the total number was doubtless great, discovered, as did David, the blessedness of the man whose iniquities are forgiven, and whose sins are covered (Rom. 4:6,7; Ps. 32:1, 2).

Now, when the purpose of the law of Sinai was fulfilled, and the era of the old covenant was ended; when the fulness of the time was come, and God sent forth His Son to accomplish "what the law could not do, in that it was weak through the flesh,"--that is, to bring man back into a state of obedience--there was need to make changes in the law of God that it might be in keeping with the new order of things about to come into existence through the work of Jesus Christ as the Mediator of the New Covenant. For Christ came to establish a Kingdom, as a hundred texts declare; and the most important feature of a kingdom, next to the occupant of the throne, is its law. But manifestly the law of God as given to an earthly people, not regenerated as a whole (though there were many regenerated persons scattered through the mass of the nation) would not be suited to a people born of God, His own children, "begotten again unto a living hope by the resurrection of Jesus Christ from the dead" (1 Pet. 1:3).

The idea that the redeemed and regenerated people of Christ were not to be "subject to the law of God" is about as far from the truth of Scripture as is possible to get. For the main object of the course of God's dealings with mankind has been that He might have a people for His name, who would obey His law from the heart. This had been made evident by certain prophecies of the Old Testament, as for example, that of Jeremiah 31:31-34, where the new covenant was distinctly foretold; and where, concerning the people that were to be embraced by that covenant, God said, "1 will put my law in their inward parts and write it in their hearts." The Epistle to the Hebrews declares that Jesus Christ is the Mediator of this new covenant (Heb. 8:6; 12:24); and that the "many sons" whom God is "bringing unto glory," through Jesus Christ, "the captain of their salvation," who is "not ashamed to call them brethren" (Heb. 2: 10, 11; 12:7-9), are the new covenant people, in whose hearts God purposed to write His law. These "many sons constitute the Kingdom of God, according to the word, "Wherefore, we receiving a kingdom which cannot be moved (shaken), let us have grace, whereby we may serve God acceptably with reverence and Godly fear" (Heb. 12:28, not referred to in the S.B.)

And likewise Isaiah, in one of his prophecies concerning this era of gospel blessing for "all nations," spoke of it as the time in which "out of Zion shall go forth the law, and the word of the Lord from Jerusalem" (Isa. 2:2-4). That "law" which was to "go forth" into all the world was the law of Christ, and that "word" was the word of the gospel of Christ. And the time of the fulfilment of this and other like prophecies is clearly fixed in the New Testament Scriptures, as where Paul spoke concerning his gospel, and the preaching of the Jesus Christ, which "now is made manifest, and by the scriptures of the PROPHETS, according to the. commandment of the everlasting God, made known to all nations for the obedience of faith" (Rom. 16:25, 26).

Therefore there were two great parts to the work that lay before the Son of God when He came into the world: First, He was to deliver the "many sons" from the dominion of sin and death; and this He did when "through death He destroyed him that had the power of death, that is the devil" (Heb. 2:14); and second, He was to give the law of God to those whom He should bring into the family of God through the door of the new birth; and this He did in His several discourses to His disciples, and chiefly in the Sermon on the Mount. And, like as Moses and the prophets added from time to time to the main body of the law originally given at Sinai, so Christ and the apostles added special revelations of the will of God for His new covenant people to the main body of the law of the Kingdom delivered by Jesus in the Sermon on the Mount.

Remembering that Moses was a type of Christ, it is instructive to note how this two-part work of Christ was pre-figured by that of Moses. For he not only brought a people out from the dominion of Pharaoh, crossing the Red Sea (typical of Christ's death and resurrection which makes a way for His people through the waters of death), but also delivered to them the law of God, which was to be for their life and welfare.

"THESE SAYINGS OF MINE"

Therefore, it is in the Sermon on the Mount (Mat. V, VI, VII) that we find the complete and formal statement of the Law of Christ, answering to the Law of Moses, given at Mount Sinai.

The contrast between the two mountains and between the attendant circumstances of these two givings of God's law to a people on earth, is wonderfully expressive of the difference between the two Covenants to which they respectively belong. At the one were awesome sights and sounds; the mountain burning with fire and quaking at the presence of God, the pealing of the trumpet long and loud, and above all that terrifying "Voice of words," which caused the people to shrink back in fright and to entreat that the word should not be spoken to them any more; "and so terrible was the sight, that Moses said, I exceedingly fear and quake." Whereas at the other mountain the same Divine Lawgiver, now in lowly human guise, sits quietly down, and the multitudes gather willingly to His feet to drink in His words; and they being thus voluntarily gathered around Him, then "He opened His mouth and taught them, saying --."

FUNDAMENTALISM VS. MODERNISM

And are those "sayings," law? Undoubtedly they are. When was there ever any question as to that? But they are the law of the New Covenant, not that of the Old Covenant; nor yet are they the law of a reconstituted Jewish kingdom of a future dispensation, as the Scofield Bible declares. This is the matter in dispute, and it is a matter of capital importance. If the reader has any doubt as to the importance of the question in dispute, let him but recall what Christ Himself said at the close of the incomparable discourse concerning the commandments which He twice designated "These Sayings of Mine." "Everyone whosoever" (for so Mat. 7:24 reads in the original text) hears those sayings of His, and doeth them is likened unto a wise man who built his house on a rock; and everyone who hears them and does them not, is likened unto a foolish man, who built his house on the sand.

Thus, the question we are now considering has to do (we have Christ's own word for it) with the foundation upon which a man builds his life structure. That is to say, it is fundamental; and hence it is (or should be) of the deepest interest to Fundamentalists. And not only so, but the "dispensational teaching" which classes these sayings of our Lord with the law of Sinai, and relegates them to a Jewish kingdom somewhere in the future, is modernism in the strictest sense, and of the most pernicious sort. Therefore what we are now discussing is of the greatest possible interest to all who profess and call themselves Fundamentalists.

Dispensationalism must inevitably fall into ruin; for it is builded upon a foundation of sand. True, the structure thereof has been ingeniously contrived and cleverly put together. Moreover, excellent materials have gone into the building of it; and the time, labor and skill of able, learned and godly men have been lavished upon the erection and adornment thereof. But it is all for nought; for it is not founded upon the words of Christ. Indeed there never was a case in which the true foundation has been so ostentatiously set aside. For the builders of this elaborate and ornate structure of doctrine, which has excited the admiration of hundreds of thousands, have openly disparaged and rejected the very "sayings" of the Son of God given by Him to serve as the foundation of our life-edifice. Therefore, the downfall of dispensationalism is but a question of time; and my conviction is that the hour is near at hand when it will be said, "and great was the fall of it."

"GOD HATH SPOKEN UNTO US"

Here is where we who are "the children of God by faith in Christ Jesus" (Gal. 3:26) must go to find the fullest statement of what our Father in heaven has spoken specially to us, and which has the greater claim to our willing and affectionate obedience because spoken by the lips of His own Son. For "God...hath in these last days spoken UNTO US BY HIS SON" (Heb 1:1, 2). And here is where we find our Lord's commandments concerning

86

which He said, "If ye love Me, keep My commandments" (John 14:15). And so it has always been held by the followers of Christ, real and nominal. Nor has it been even supposed before our times that there could be any other view of the matter. But now it is dogmatically taught, and without rebuke, in the very midst of the most orthodox groups of Christians, in Bible schools and at Bible conferences, that "The Sermon on the Mount is law and not grace"; indeed that it is "law, and that raised to its highest, most deathful, and destructive potency." Think of such expressions being applied to our Lord's Sermon on the Mount!

A BIT OF RECENT HISTORY

In the year 1918 I published a little book ("The Kingdom of Heaven: What is it?") in which I pointed out that the Sermon on the Mount carries in its own text the clearest evidence that it is a message from God the Father to His own children; since again and again Christ speaks of "thy Father," "your Father," your heavenly Father"; and He there teaches them how they shall act "that ye may be the children of your Father in heaven," and to pray, saying, "Our Father, Who art in heaven." And I pointed out that, in the notes of the Scofield Bible, the fact that Christ gives in His Sermon on the Mount the Father's words to His own "children"--a fact which certainly is decisive of the issues we are discussing--is wholly ignored. Dr. Scofield felt called upon to take some notice of this; so he published shortly thereafter a magazine article under the caption "Is the Sermon on the Mount Law?" And so willing was I (as I still am) that both sides should be heard, that I published Dr. Scofield's article in full with some comments of my own. [2] The following is the first paragraph of Dr. Scofield's article:

"For the first time in nearly two thousand years of study and discussion of revealed truth, the statement has recently been made that the Sermon on the Mount is not Law. The times are noisy with novelties of every description, and especially in the sphere of Bible truth. If this particular novelty stood alone, it might, more safely than any others, be left to break itself against the very phrasing of that great declaration."

Needless to say I had never stated or implied that "the Sermon on the Mount is not law." The question I had raised in my book above referred to was stated thus:

"The question is, to whom are those words (the Sermon on the Mount) spoken? Are they spoken directly to, and to be heeded by, the people of God of this dispensation? Or are they spoken to Jews of some past or future era, with possibly an indirect 'moral application' to us?"

Yet, in replying to that book, the best that Dr. Scofield could do was to ignore the real question altogether, and to confine himself to the discussion of a question which never had been raised. And he proceeds to say that "the times are noisy with novelties of every description, and especially in the sphere of Bible truth," and to place the view he was supposedly answering in the category of those noisy novelties, thus completely reversing the actual situation, in which the "novelty" (whether "noisy" or otherwise) is beyond all dispute the view advanced by Dr. Scofield.

Thus the matter stands to-day as it stood then.

NOT OF WORKS

To some the doctrine of Christ as given in the Sermon on the Mount, presents a difficulty in that it does not expressly declare that a man's salvation depends upon his faith, not upon his works; according as it was subsequently written by the apostle Paul, "For by grace ye are saved, through faith; and that not of yourselves, it is the gift of God; not of works, lest any man should boast" (Eph. 2:8, 9).

But there is no difficulty here; for the Sermon on the Mount was not spoken to explain how a man gets the new birth and enters into the Kingdom of God, but to teach those who had already entered into that Kingdom how to act as becometh those who are saved by grace through faith and have the knowledge of God the Father through the Son.

Christ had previously explained to Nicodemus, a teacher of the Jews, that entrance into the Kingdom of God was only by the narrow way of the new birth--a thing possible to God alone--and that for man, the only condition of salvation was to believe in Him whom God had sent into the world, His Son (John 3:5, 14-18). And this vital truth is stated also in the Sermon on the Mount; for there we read:

"Enter ye in at the strait gate: for wide is the gate and broad is the way that leadeth to destruction, and many there be which go in thereat. Because strait is the gate and narrow is the way which leadeth unto life; and few there be that find it" (Mat. 7:12, 13).

And this, in the Lord's wisdom, was deemed enough on that subject for the purpose of that discourse and for the permanent record of it that was to become a part of the New Testament Scriptures which were not written and collected for nearly a generation later. For, in order to be saved, a man needs not to understand the conditions of salvation, or to know anything about the new birth. The one condition he must fulfil is to believe in the Lord Jesus Christ. And these words on the Mount were spoken to "His disciples," those who "came unto Him," and who thus manifested their faith in Him; though doubtless there were among them some who were moved by motives other than faith, and to these the warning given in the above quoted words was needful.

The Sermon on the Mount therefore presupposes that the hearers are already the people of God having entered the Kingdom of God in the only way it can be entered.

For here we have another point of resemblance between Moses, the mediator of the old covenant, and Jesus Christ, the mediator of the new, of whom Moses spoke when he said:

"The Lord thy God will raise up unto thee a Prophet from the midst of thee, of thy brethren, like unto me; unto Him shall ye hearken, according unto all that thou desiredst of the Lord thy God in Horeb,...saying, Let me not hear again the voice of the Lord my God, neither let me see this great fire any more, that I die not. And the Lord said unto me, They have well spoken that which they have spoken. I will raise them up a Prophet from among their brethren, like unto thee, and will put My words in His mouth; and He shall speak unto them all that I shall command thee." (Deut. 18:14-18).

Christ was a Prophet like unto Moses in that (among other points of resemblance) He spoke the words of God to a people whom God had set apart for Himself. And just as the law of Mount Sinai was given to, and intended to be obeyed by, a people whom God had delivered out of Egypt, from under the yoke of Pharaoh, and brought through the waters of the Red Sea; even so, the law of that other Mount is given for the obedience of a people delivered out of this present evil world, from under the yoke of its prince, and brought through the waters of death and judgment by the death and resurrection of Jesus Christ.

The Sermon on the Mount was not spoken to the promiscuous multitudes on the plain below, the "sick people," those "taken with divers diseases and torments, and those which were possessed with devils, and those which were lunatic, and those that had the palsy"; whom He healed; and because of which "there followed Him great multitudes of people from Galilee," and from other regions, some quite remote (Mat. 4:24, 25). Those great multitudes saw His miracles and received temporal benefits; but they did not hear the Sermon on the Mount. To enjoy that unspeakable privilege they must have the heart of a disciple, and must undergo the exertion of climbing the mountain. For "Seeing the multitudes, He went up into a mountain: and when He was set His disciples came unto Him; and He opened His mouth, and taught them." And then proceeded from His gracious lips (Psa. 45:2) those matchless "words of grace," which God had promised through Moses when He said, "And I will put My words IN HIS MOUTH."

The Word of God records for our instruction the two great and wonderful occasions in the history of the world when men heard the Voice of God Himself uttering the commandments which they were to keep. What a marvellous contrast there is between those two occasions! I have already made a brief reference to that great contrast; but it is highly important that we note carefully the difference, and ascertain the reason therefor.

At Mount Sinai there were terrifying sights and sounds; for the mount was altogether on a smoke, because the Lord descended upon it in fire; and the whole mount quaked greatly. There were, moreover, blackness and darkness and tempest, and the sound of the trumpet, which sounded long and waxed louder and louder. But hardest of all for them to bear was that "Voice of words," the Voice of the Lord which is powerful and full of majesty, which so filled them with terror that they entreated that the Word should not be spoken unto them any more. As it is written (Ex. 20:18, 19):

"And all the people saw the thunderings, and the lightnings, and the noise of the trumpet, and the mountain smoking: and when the people saw, they removed and stood afar off. And they said unto Moses, Speak thou with us and we will hear: but let not God speak with us, lest we die."

How different it was at the other mountain, concerning which it is written (Matt. 5:1):

"And seeing the multitudes, He went up into a mountain: and when He was set,

His disciples came unto Him"!

Why did they come to Him now, and not remove and stand far off as when the same Lord gave commandments to an earthly people at Mount Sinai? Why did they climb that mountain and listen unterrified to His words? He was not working miracles on the mountain, nor dispensing loaves and fishes; but was giving commandments, even as at the other mountain; yet "His disciples came unto Him" and quietly listened while He brought them into known relations with the Father Who had sent Him for this very ministry.

There is much to be learned from this wonderful contrast; but we can only indicate briefly the leading points; and the most important is that, in these two contrasted scenes, we have the main differences between the two eras to which they respectively belong. In one we see man shrinking from the presence and the voice of God, and standing "afar off." This is "LAW." In the other we have Immanuel, God the Saviour, come in the lowly guise of sinful flesh, associating Himself with sinners, in order to bring them into the closest and holiest relations with Himself. This is "GRACE."

Furthermore we see the character of the era of grace in the fact that the disciples' coming to Him was voluntary. It was their own heart that prompted them to ascend that mountain and listen to His Words. The

Lord met the needs of "the multitudes" on the low levels of the plain; but those only who were drawn to His own Person up to the mountain-top, received of His words. To those who respond to the gospel He gives "rest" from the burden and penalty of sin; and to them He also says: "Take My yoke upon you and learn of Me"; but He does not force His yoke upon any, nor compel even His own people to learn of Him. It is pure grace.

As we think on these things and meditate upon the great work of grace which has been going on for nineteen centuries with so little outward show, we can see with the mind's eye the "many children" newly born into the Kingdom of heaven hastening, in response to a heaven-sent impulse, up the mountain, away from the distracting sights and sounds of the earth, to that quiet place where Christ's own voice may be heard speaking the words His Father gave Him to speak (John 7:16; 17:8). But a strange thing has come to pass in our days. Heretofore those who were recognized and trusted as leaders among God's people did all they could to encourage the young believers to take Christ's yoke, and to submit to His commandments, assuring them, in the words of the apostle John, that "His commandments are not grievous." But now, alas that such a thing should be! There are men of learning and ability, esteemed widely as sound and safe expositors of Scripture, who make it their business to hinder those of the household of faith who would go up the mountain where Christ's own words are to be heard; and who tell them in the most positive terms that those words are not for God's children at all, but for some "Jewish disciples" of another era. And who, after having represented the law of God as a thing to be feared and shunned, declared that the Sermon on the Mount is "Law raised to its highest, most deathful and destructive potency"!

In time past the obstacles in the way of one who would press up the mountain in order to be in the presence of his Lord and to receive "the doctrine of Christ" from His own lips, were such as might appeal to the natural heart. The world spread its attractions before the eye, and the flesh raised itself up against the exertion required for the ascent. But now the case is far more serious; for we find men of the strictest orthodoxy who have posted themselves in the way in order to intercept any of the children whom they may find heading for that Mount of nine times "Blessed" ones; and we hear these teachers saying in the most authoritative tones that the mountain and the words of Him Who there speaks from heaven belong not to this dispensation of grace at all; that it is "legal ground"; that the Father's words are "Jewish," being the "principle" of a far-off earthly kingdom; and that the early Christians who "grounded themselves" on those words were a "dangerous sect"! What a shame! What a deep dishonor to the throne of God! And what a cruel wrong to unsuspecting babes in Christ, who are thus turned away from the words given to them as "the Rock" whereon to build a life-structure that will endure! Brethren, let us pray for these men, that God will indeed give them repentance unto the acknowledging of the truth; and also that Christ's "little ones" may be rescued from this new danger. Well did the apostle say that in the last days "perilous times" should come.

The Lord Jesus Christ, as First-born over the entire family of God, shares everything He has with the beloved children. And among the choicest of those family possessions are the Father's "commandments." Speaking of these He said: "I have kept My Father's commandments and abide in His love" (John 15:10); and again, "That the world may know that I love the Father, and as the Father gave Me commandment, even so I do" (id. 14:31). By these, and by many other Scriptures, we learn that the Kingdom of heaven calls upon those who are in it to keep the commandments of God willingly, and through love alone. But, according to this new teaching, the doing of the Father's commandments is "legality." [3] If therefore our hearts respond at all to the grace of God manifested to us in bringing us into His household on the footing of children, then we shall not be looking for excuses to justify ourselves in not keeping His commandments, but on the contrary we shall be rather eager to keep them; we shall count it a privilege to have them; they will be our joy, our treasure, our chief delight; and the law of His mouth will be better to us than thousands of gold and silver.

Let me here mention another fact which proves conclusively that the Sermon on the Mount belongs, and exclusively, to this present era of grace. For that message is manifestly for those people of God who find themselves in conditions which exist in this present era and none other. An attentive reader of these chapters (Matthew V, VI, VII) cannot fail to see that the circumstances of those addressed are precisely what God's children have to face in this age; and that it is simply an impossibility to fit the discourse into the conditions that will exist on earth after the second coming of Christ.

The Lord tells those to whom this Sermon is given that they are "the light of the world," and that they are to let their light shine; which is just what the apostles wrote later to the church (Eph. 5:8; Phil. 2:15; Jam. 1:17; 1 Pet. 2:9). In the age to come the Lord Himself will be the Light of the world, which will be filled with His glory. In the Sermon on the Mount He further says that His people will be persecuted and reviled for His Name's sake; that they are to submit to evil, to turn the other cheek when smitten; that they are to be reviled and hated and exposed to false PROPHETS. Those conditions prevail during this age of His rejection and absence; but will be wholly abolished when He comes again.

Furthermore, a large and important section of the Sermon is devoted to the subject of care and anxiety regarding the necessities of this life--food and clothing. It is in this present age of the Lord's absence, and in none other, that His people have to undergo trials of faith in regard to these needful things, and find themselves exposed to anxious care for the morrow. It is manifestly impossible to fit the sixth chapter of Matthew into any age but this; and we have yet to see the first attempt to do so. This is pre-eminently and conspicuously the age in which the god of riches, the mammon of unrighteousness, competes with God Himself for the love and confidence of His people. Indeed, if we had only the words "lay not up for yourselves treasures on earth, but lay up for yourselves treasures in heaven to enlighten us, we would be able to see clearly that the Sermon on the Mount is not "Jewish," but for a heavenly people. The idea that these commandments of Christ are intended for a Kingdom of Jewish prosperity and world-supremacy for which the carnally minded Jews were (and are) looking, and which, according to "dispensational teaching," is to follow this gospel age, is not only contrary to the Word of God, but is grotesquely absurd.

DOING THE WILL OF GOD FROM THE HEART

But we have digressed from our subject; so we come back to the great truth that salvation is by grace alone through faith. And let it be noted that this is true not in this era only, but in every other as well. But God demands that the faith shall be real; and the proof of real faith is obedience, loyal loving submission to the revealed will of God. Therefore, that the members of the church at Corinth were saved was manifested by their "professed subjection unto the gospel of Christ" (2 Cor. 9:13). And therefore the doctrine of Christ contained in Matthew VII, while it affirms the foundation truth that salvation is only by faith in Himself, puts the strongest emphasis upon the fact that true faith manifests itself as such, and also builds for its possessor an enduring structure, in the doing of the will of God as revealed in those "sayings" of His Son.

Therefore what is most needful for us to understand, whom God has delivered from the power of darkness and translated into the Kingdom of His dear Son, is that the obedience upon which the Lord so strongly insists in that great utterance, is--not the effort of the natural man to keep the law of God (a thing which God plainly says is impossible, Rom. 8:7), but--the spontaneous desire and purpose of the renewed heart to do the good and acceptable and perfect will of God. For in this is the essence of Christ-likeness; and hence it is the nature of the "new man" and the outcome of the new birth.

It is not, of course, demanded as a condition of final salvation that the child of God shall be manifesting in all his acts and words the character of the Obedient One; for none other could say, "1 delight to do Thy will, O my God; yea, Thy law is within my heart" (Psa. 40:8). For it is a truth of Scripture, and of the humbling experience also of every child of God, that the "old man" remains still in those who have been born of God, and his hateful ways are all too frequently seen in their behavior. But on the other hand, if the "obedience of Christ" is never seen in one who professes the faith of Christ, it is proof that there has never been a work of God in his heart. For when the disciples came to Jesus asking, "Who is the greatest in the kingdom of heaven?" He called a little child unto 1-lim, and setting him before them as an object lesson, He said: "Verily, I say unto you, Except ye be converted" (a work of God) "and become as little children, ye shall not enter into the kingdom of heaven" (Mat. 18:1-3).

BY THEIR FRUITS

Furthermore, in the verses of the Sermon on the Mount immediately following those in which Christ speaks of entering in at the strait gate, He uses another illustration which serves to make His meaning clearer. In those verses (Mat. 7:15-20), He points out that fruit is the product of life (and hence the evidence of it) ; and that the character of the fruit depends entirely upon the character of the tree. This goes to the very root of the matter. It declares in the strongest way that a corrupt tree cannot bring forth good fruit. It is an impossibility. What then? Seeing that every man is by nature utterly corrupt, how can anyone bring forth the fruits of good deeds? The Lord Himself has given the answer, saying, "Make the tree good, and his fruit good" (Mat. 12:33); and the context shows (v. 35) that he is speaking of the heart of man. In other words, one must be born again, and receive the Holy Spirit, ere he can produce the fruit of the Spirit (Gal. 3:26; 4:6; 5:22, 23).

We find then that the doctrine of Christ, as given in the concluding portion of the Sermon on the Mount. so far from being in conflict with the truth of the gospel, sets forth that truth in the clearest light. The gospel demands obedience; and it is preached for the express purpose of producing obedience among all nations, even "the obedience of faith" (Rom. 1:5; 6:17; 15:18; 16:19, 26). Indeed "eternal destruction from the presence of the Lord" is to be the portion of all who "obey not the gospel of our Lord Jesus Christ" (2 Th. 1:7-9).

Hence the first question of one who has been saved by grace is that which Saul of Tarsus asked: "Lord, what wilt Thou have me to do?" One who sincerely asks this question has been already saved by grace through faith; and such a one will find a full, though concise, answer to his question in the Sermon on the Mount. And to "these sayings" he will go, not to gain salvation by the keeping of them; but, knowing that his salvation is already secured by the work of Christ and the Holy Spirit, making him a child of God, he will go to them in order that, in the doing of them, he may let his light so shine before men that they may see his good works and glorify his Father who is in heaven.

Notes

1. It is well to remember, when we hear the law of God thus spoken of, that it is the "carnal mind" that is being permitted to express itself. For the spiritual mind loves the law of God, and is even at a loss to find words to express its admiration for it, and its "delight" in it. But the very mention of the law of God stirs up the enmity of the carnal mind. The thought of being under it is intolerable. It cannot bear the contemplation of such a thing; because it is "not subject to the law of God, neither indeed can be."

2. See "Is the Sermon on the Mount Law? by C. I. Scofield; with Comments by P. Mauro." Hamilton Bros. 10c.

3. In the article by Dr. Scofield to which reference has been made above, it is stated that any one who teaches that the Sermon on the Mount is for the children of God is a "Legalizer," of the same sort as those who taught in apostolic times that the Gentile disciples must be circumcised and keep the law of Moses in order to be saved, and concerning whom the apostle Paul said "Let him be accursed," as the preacher of "another (i.e. a different) gospel." We have therefore a startling contrast to which close heed should be given, for it presents the issue in a striking way: The Lord says of His commandments in the Sermon on the Mount that "Whosoever shall do and teach them, the same shall be called 'great' in the Kingdom of heaven"; but the editor says the same shall be called a "Legalizer," and be liable to the curse referred to.

Chapter Eleven - The Character of the Sermon on the Mount

MY main purpose in the present chapter is to show more fully than has yet been done in the preceding pages that the Sermon on the Mount exhibits in every part thereof the character of grace.

There is the utmost need of making this clear and plain to the people of God because the new popular "Bible" whose teachings we are examining declares in the most unqualified way that - "The Sermon on the Mount is law, not grace"; and that "The doctrines of grace are to be sought in the Epistles, not in the Gospels" (Ed. of 1909, p. 989).

Further it is stated in the "Bible" referred to that --

"The Sermon on the Mount in its primary application gives neither the privilege nor the duty of the church" (id., p. 1000).

And again that - "It is evident that the really dangerous sect in Corinth was that which said 'I am of Christ.' They rejected the new revelation through Paul of the doctrine of grace; grounding themselves probably on the kingdom teachings of our Lord" (id., p. 1230).

It will be seen that, in the last of the above quotations from the "Scofield Bible," not only is the teaching of Paul set in contrast with, and made to appear as a superior to, that of the Lord Jesus Christ, but the latter is exhibited as that which lays a foundation--not for a true Christian life and character as the Lord Him-self declared, but--for a "really dangerous sect." Could anything be more subversive of vital truth or fraught with greater possibilities for danger and loss to the household of faith? Is it not therefore the urgent duty of every one who has a thought for the honor of the Lord Jesus Christ and the welfare of His people to cry out against this novel and destructive teaching, and against the "Bible" which contains it?

For what are the points of the doctrine of Christ contained in the Sermon on the Mount? These are the principle ones:

1.   To let our light shine before men for the glory of our Father in heaven.
2.   To refrain from the angry thought and word, and from the impure desire and look.
3.   To submit to injury.
4.   To give, to lend, to love our enemies.
5.   To return blessing for cursing, to do good and to pray for those who do us harm.
6.   To be like our Father in heaven.
7.   To seek not a reputation for piety or almsgiving, like the Pharisees.
8.   To give God's things the first and largest place in our prayers.
9.   To forgive without limit all trespasses against ourselves.
10.   To lay up treasures in heaven, not on earth.
11.   To serve God and not Mammon.
12.   To trust our heavenly Father for the needful things of this life, taking no anxious thought for the morrow.
13.   To seek first the Kingdom of God and His righteousness.
14.   To refrain from judging our brethren; and, in a word, to do to others whatsoever we would that men should do to us.

Such is "the doctrine of Christ," concerning which the apostle John says: "He that abideth in the doctrine of Christ, he hath both the FATHER and the SON" (comp. the Lord's words in John 14:23) ; and, "If there come any unto you, and bring not THIS DOCTRINE, receive him not into your house, neither bid him God speed" (2 John 9, 10). This is the "doctrine" concerning which the editor of the "Scofield Bible" says that they who grounded themselves upon it were "the really dangerous sect" at Corinth; and concerning which he also says in another publication ("Our Hope" December, 1919), "The Sermon on the Mount is law, and that raised to its highest, most deathful and destructive potency." What terrible words are these! Surely the first nine verses of the Sermon, the "Beatitudes," are quite enough to refute this false and injurious statement, and to show that the discourse pertains not to the curse of the law but to the free blessings of the gospel.

We ask careful attention now to the grace of God as marvelously displayed in the Sermon on the Mount; and after that we will examine the reasons which the editor of the Scofield Bible has brought forward in support of his statement that the Sermon on the Mount is "not grace" but "law, and that raised to its highest, most deathful and destructive potency"--a thing to be feared and shunned.

First. The quality of purest grace is seen in the Sermon on the Mount in that the Son of God is therein bringing sinful men into the knowledge of the Father, and into the conscious enjoyment of the relationship, the privileges and the responsibilities of the children of God. Not only is this grace, but it may be said without fear of contradiction that grace can do no more for sinful men than to bring them into the family of God on the footing of children.

The One Who, in this marvellous utterance, brings those who were by nature aliens and enemies of God into intimate and holy relations with God the Father, is the very One Who had to come to offer that Sacrifice without which such relationship would have been forever an impossibility; without which there would have been nothing for the best of men but death and judgment and the lake of fire. Hence the whole discourse assumes the work of Redemption to have been accomplished. We do not find in it any explanation of the means by which those addressed would be made the children of God; but such explanation is not called for in the address in the form given to it as a part of the written Word. In that form it is for those who have come to Christ the crucified and risen One in response to the gospel, and who know already the ground of their acceptance with God. We are not told just what explanations on this point the Lord gave in His oral teaching; but we know that "when they were alone He expounded all things to His disciples" (Mk. 4:34).

Second. The quality of divine grace is also conspicuously exhibited in the Sermon on the Mount in that those who are there addressed are made the Children of God without works or merit on their part. We have here the greatest possible contrast between God's dealings with the Israelites at Mt. Sinai, and His dealings with the objects of His grace in this dispensation. The position or relationship offered to the children of Israel of Mt. Sinai was expressly conditioned upon their obedience. The offer was made in these words: --

"Now, therefore, if ye will obey My voice indeed, and keep My covenant, then ye shall be a peculiar treasure unto Me above all people; for all the earth is Mine; and ye shall be to Me a kingdom of priests and an holy nation."

And thereupon -- "All the people answered together and said, All that the Lord hath spoken we will do" (Ex. 19:5-8).

That covenant was, as we know, flagrantly broken by all the people; and hence it became null and void. It is idle therefore to say that God was under any obligation whatever to "offer" to Israel and any "kingdom" at any time. His purpose for that people, as for all men, must, from the breaking of that covenant, be carried out upon the basis of grace alone.

But, in contrast with the conditional covenant which God made at Mount Sinai with the children of Israel. no conditions whatever are made with the children of God to whom Christ gives His teaching on the Mount; and, if we know the most elementary truths concerning God's dealings with men, we know that this is the great distinguishing difference between law and grace. [1] The Lord Jesus Christ, in His Sermon on the mount, speaks to "children" of God, with never a word of anything to be done by them to bring them into that relationship, or to maintain them therein. Hence one can fail to see "grace" as distinguished from "law" in this discourse only by closing his eyes to that which is most conspicuously exhibited in it. We know that there is but one way a man can become a child of God, namely by the new birth which is the gift of grace to all who believe in Jesus Christ. We know, too, that, although His own people as a nation "received Him not," yet some individuals did receive Him; and that to "as many as received Him to them GAVE He the power (right or privilege) to become the sons (children) of God, even to them that believe on His Name, who were born...of God" (John 1:11-13). It was to those who "received Him," and to whom by grace it was given to become children of God, that the Father's instructions (the Sermon on the Mount) were spoken: and hence that utterance became, and is, the abiding Rock-foundation upon which the members of God's great family are, one and all, to build. This is as plain as words can make it. It follows that they who, for whatever motive and by whatever means, seek to deprive the children of God of the Sermon on the Mount, are striking at the Foundation upon which their all is to be built. Can anything be more serious?

Third. Grace is further displayed in the Sermon on the Mount in the nature of the motive or inducement offered for the doing of the things commanded therein. For example, our light is to shine in the darkness of this world, not in order that God may see our good works and bless us by making us His children, but that men may see them and glorify our Father Who is in heaven, and Who has already made us His children. We are "to do and teach" these commandments, not that we may thereby gain entrance into the Kingdom of heaven, but that (having been brought into it by grace) we may be "called great" therein. We are to love our enemies, to bless them that curse us, etc., not in order to gain a place in the family of God, but because, having been freely given that place of highest privilege, we are to be (in all our behaviour) what God has made us. The lesson is precisely that given to the household of God by the apostle Paul in the words: "Be ye, therefore, followers (imitators) of God as beloved children; and walk in love as Christ also hath loved us" (Eph. 5:1, 2).

Grace is seen then in the position of eternal dignity and glory into which the Lord Jesus lifts those to whom this message from God the Father was sent. Grace is further seen in the fact that the position of nearness to God known and enjoyed only by the Son Himself is given to guilty rebels freely, without any works on their part. And grace is still further seen in that the commands which the Father here gives to His children afford opportunity to them to gain rich rewards; whereas failure on their part, while it will entail suffering and loss (as all the New Testament teaches), will not involve the forfeiture of their relationship with God.

In view of all this clear truth, what possible reasons can the wit of man devise for setting aside the Sermon on the Mount as "legal," and as having no proper place or part in the dispensation of grace? Is it because it contains commandments? So the editor seems to contend in the article from which I have quoted above. But the Epistles of Paul are full of "the commandments of the Lord," as everyone knows who has read them.2 And surely we should all be astonished at any one who would dare assert that it is not in keeping with "grace" for the Father to give commandments to His own children. Would it not be a disgrace to any human father who should fail in that duty? And are we who are, by grace alone, the children of God to refuse every message from Him which demands obedience, and which puts before us the consequences of disobedience? If so, then there are no Scriptures for us, and nothing for us to do in this life but to please ourselves. It is almost unbelievable that anyone would advance such a proposition; yet we have to take notice of the fact that Dr. Scofield, in the article last referred to, argues that the Sermon on the Mount is not for us because it is "couched in the language of authority, rather than in the language of kindly counsel"; and because "nowhere is the phrasing that of good advice, but always imperative requirement." This certainly implies that our Father in heaven is not permitted to speak to His children in "the language of authority" (though He bids earthly parents thus to command their children and to enforce obedience with the rod), but only in the "language of kindly counsel" and in the phrasing of "good advice." Surely there is no need to discuss such a proposition.

This brings us to the passage by which the editor, both in his "Bible" and his published articles, seeks to support the statement that "the Sermon on the Mount is law and not grace." That passage is Matthew 6:12, 14, 15, which reads as follows: --

"And forgive us our debts, as we forgive our debtors...For if ye forgive men their trespasses, your heavenly Father will also forgive you: But if ye forgive not men their trespasses, neither will your Father forgive your trespasses."

Upon this the editor's note says: "This is legal ground. Cf. Eph. 4:32, which is grace. Under law forgiveness is conditioned upon a like spirit in us: under grace we are forgiven for Christ's sake and exhorted to forgive because we have been forgiven."

And in the article referred to above he says that in the Sermon on the Mount "Every blessing is conditional upon works, not faith."

I have already amply shown that this last statement is directly contrary to the truth. We have, therefore, only to inquire, is Matthew 6:12-15 "legal ground"? and if so does it follow that the entire Sermon on the Mount belongs to another "dispensation"?

In regard to these questions I submit as follows, taking them in reverse order:

1. Whatever view may be taken of the words of Matthew 6:12-15, the main question as to the "dispensational" place of the Sermon on the Mount remains unaffected. For I have shown by the clearest proofs that the message is the Father's message to His own children. Hence if we find anything "legal" in that message we must conclude that it properly belongs there. For the children to reject their Father's commandment because it contains a clause which they choose to regard as "legal," would be a most presumptuous thing.

2. I maintain, however, that the words of the passage in question are not only consistent with God's grace in making believing sinners His children, but that they tend to emphasize strongly the fact that the

Kingdom to which the Sermon on the Mount pertains is that of grace. For it is clear that the conspicuous feature of this day of grace is the forgiveness of sins, which is preached in the Name of Jesus Christ and on the ground of His atoning Sacrifice, to all the world. Hence everyone who enters the Kingdom of God is a forgiven sinner. He has been fully and freely pardoned and justified from all things. Therefore, he is required, and most properly required--seeing that the character of the Kingdom into which God's grace has brought him imperatively demands it--to forgive others their "debts" or "trespasses" against himself. The passage has nothing whatever to do with the man's sins, which were all forgiven when he was made a child of God. It relates to a very different matter, that of debts or trespasses; and it is truly an amazing thing that any one who considers himself fitted to comment upon the whole Bible should fail to distinguish between things so widely different in their nature as God's forgiveness of the repentant sinner and the Father's forgiveness of the trespasses of His own children. [2]

It is a truth of great practical importance for every child of God to know that if he, who has received by grace the free pardon of all his sins, should refuse to forgive the "trespasses" of others against himself (the greatest of which would be a relatively trifling thing), he will be left now in this present life to the consequences of his own "trespasses" (and does not everyone of us know by experience something of what that means?) with the possibility of future loss besides.

I feel bound, moreover, to enter the most serious objection to the statement that "under the law of the kingdom no one may hope for forgiveness who has not first forgiven." Even in the dispensation of law God did not deal with men on that basis. One needs but slight knowledge of Scripture to be aware that God ever and always forgave the penitent sinner upon confession and faith alone. THERE NEVER HAS BEEN, IS NOT NOW, NOR EVER WILL BE, BUT ONE BASIS UPON WHICH GOD FORGIVES THE SINNER; and we are bound to protest that it not only assails the foundation truth of Redemption, but also does deep dishonor to the Lord Jesus Christ, to say that in the Kingdom announced and introduced by Himself no one may hope for forgiveness who has not first forgiven. For David lived during the era of the law, yet he is conspicuously the man who knew by experience the blessedness of those "whose iniquities are forgiven and whose sins are covered" (Rom. 4:6, 7). The very coats of skin, wherewith God in His pardoning mercy covered the nakedness of the first pair of sinners, bore witness to the eternal truth that without the shedding of blood there is no remission of sins.

The words of Matthew 6:12 are of immense practical value; for if we use the prayer-pattern "given by the Lord (not as a form, but as a pattern) praying in our closets "after this manner," the clause "as we forgive our debtors" will cause us to search our hearts in His very presence for any unforgiving or resentful thought ere we can seek or expect to enjoy the forgiveness of our own trespasses.

Near the end of our Lord's ministry--long after the kingdom had been "postponed" according to the editor's theory--He repeated this lesson, saying:

"Therefore I say unto you, What things soever ye desire when ye pray, believe that ye receive them, and ye shall have them. And when ye stand praying forgive, if ye have ought against any; that your Father also which is in heaven may forgive you your trespasses. But if ye do not forgive, neither will your Father which is in heaven forgive your trespasses" (Mark 11:24-26).

The editor cannot, consistently with his own teaching, assign these words of the Lord to the category of His "kingdom teachings," for they were spoken but a few days before His death. Hence the same doctrine found in the Sermon on the Mount cannot, even by the editor's own theory, mark it as belonging to the dispensation of law. On what then does the theory rest? Clearly it is entirely destitute of support.

To sum up: there is an important difference between the sinner's sins and the believer's trespasses. The sinner, when he comes to Christ, receives the forgiveness of all his sins through the merit of Christ's atoning Sacrifice, and upon the sole condition of "repentance toward God and faith toward our Lord Jesus Christ." The believer's trespasses, committed after he has been forgiven and accepted as a child of God, are forgiven through confession (1 John 1:9), through the intercession of the Advocate, Jesus Christ the Righteous at God's right hand (1 John 2:2), and upon the ground of the same Sacrifice. The believer, however, cannot count upon this forgiveness of his trespasses (but on the contrary may expect to suffer the consequences of them) if he refuses or fails to forgive the trespasses of others against himself. It is with this matter that our Lord's teaching, which we have examined in this chapter, has to do.

Notes

1. According to Rom. 6:14 and other Scriptures, to he "under law" means to be in the servitude or "dominion" of sin, and hence liable to the penalty of sin; for the law could do nothing with or for the sinner but to consign him to the penalty righteously due him. Hence sin has dominion over those who are "under the law." But "under grace" a remedy for sin has been provided through Jesus Christ; and they who are under grace can and should keep the commandments of God "from the heart" (v. 17).

2. For example, in the Epistle to the Romans from Chapter 12:1 to Chapter 15:7, are commandments of the Lord for those who are in His Kingdom; and in the midst of these laws is the inspired definition (already quoted) of "the Kingdom of God" (Rom. 14:17).

Chapter Twelve - The Kingdom of God Coming with Power

THREE of the Gospels record a prophecy of Christ concerning His Kingdom, which, by His express word, was to be fulfilled in the lifetime of some who heard it. This is Mark's record of it:

"Verily I say unto you, that there be some of them that stand here which shall not taste of death, till they have seen the kingdom of God come with power" (Mark 9:1).

Matthew records the same prediction, but with a slight variation of language, the time of the predicted event being stated thus: "Till they see the Son of Man coming in His Kingdom" (Mat. 16:28). In Luke it reads: "Till they see the kingdom of God" (Luke 9:27).

Have we then the authentic record of any event happening within that generation that answers to this prediction? There were two happenings that claim attention as we seek an answer to this question. Both those happenings were of great importance in the accomplishment of God's revealed purposes concerning His Kingdom, and both occurred within the time so emphatically limited by our Lord's words.

Those two events were, first the coming of the Holy Spirit on the day of Pentecost; and second, the destruction of Jerusalem and of the Jewish nation by the Romans in A.D. 70. Each of these events may be regarded, and without straining at all the meaning of the words, as a coming of the Kingdom of God. And each, moreover, may be regarded, in the light of Scripture, as a coining of that Kingdom with attendant circumstances that answer to the phrase "with power"; circumstances such as were absent during Christ's earthly ministry.

For the outpouring of the Holy Spirit was unquestionably a coming of that Kingdom which the apostle Paul afterwards defined as "Righteousness, and peace, and joy in the Holy Ghost" (Rom. 14:17). We recall, moreover, in regard to the phrase "With power," that our Lord, in speaking to His disciples concerning the then approaching advent of the Holy Ghost, had said, "Ye shall receive power" (Acts 1:8). Power was needed and was promised for the effective preaching of that gospel whereby those who believe it are translated into the Kingdom of God's dear Son" (Col. 1:12, 13); that gospel which is "the power of God unto salvation to every one that believeth" (Rom. 1:16).

The appalling destruction of the Jewish nation, their beautiful city and their magnificent temple--which unprecedented catastrophe was described anticipatively by Christ Himself (Mat. XXIV, Mark XIII, Luke XXI)--was likewise a most evident and impressive coming of the Son of man "in power." It was a coming in final judgment upon that nation; and its awful details prefigure the final judgment of the world.

Unhappily the significance of that world-shaking event is greatly minimized in the teaching of our day. And my conviction is that, unless one sees the destruction of Jerusalem by the Romans and the events attending and consequent upon it in their true relation to the whole scheme of God's dealings with the human race in its two divisions of Jews and Gentiles, he will not be able to understand the general purport of Bible prophecy.

Of the two events referred to above as possible fulfilments of our Lord's prophecy, one occurred within a year of the time the prophecy was uttered, whereas the other lay much farther in the future--about forty years. Nevertheless, some who were standing there, notably the apostle John, lived to "see" that great work of divine "power" and judgment, which Moses had foretold (Deut. 28:49-64), and the like of which had not been "since the beginning of the world" (Mat. 24:21).

After much deliberation upon the matter, my conclusion is that, if choice must be made between those two events, it is the one later in date--that is, the annihilation of the Jewish nation, that being the manifest taking away from them of the Kingdom of God (according to the word of Christ recorded in Matthew 21:43)--that our Lord had in view when He uttered the prophecy we are considering. I will indicate, in what follows, my main reasons for so thinking.

1. The words, "There be some standing here that shall not taste of death" indicate that He had in contemplation an event that lay at a considerable distance in the future relatively to the ordinary duration of human life. His reference to the death of some then standing by would hardly be appropriate with respect to an event that was to happen within the space of a year.

2. But a stronger reason is found in our Lord's Olivet prophecy, which is recorded by each of the three Gospel-writers who record the prophecy spoken at Caesarea Philippi. For in Christ's Olivet prophecy, the desolation of Judea, the siege of Jerusalem, the demolition of the Temple, and the world-wide dispersion of the Jewish people, were foretold in detail. Specially is it to be observed that our Lord made use in that

prophecy of expressions that are strikingly similar to those used in the earlier prophecy. Thus, referring in the Olivet prophecy to the approaching desolation of Judea and Jerusalem, He said, "Verily I say unto you, this generation shall not pass until all these things be fulfilled" (Mat. 24:34). Manifestly the words I have italicised are the exact equivalent of "There be some standing here which shall not taste of death till --" Moreover, in each case we have the emphatic introductory clause, "Verily I say unto you." Furthermore, the preceding chapter records the judgment pronounced upon the leaders of the nation, whereof the closing words are, "Verily I say unto you, "All these things shall come upon this generation" (Mat. 23:36). And then follows His sore lament for Jerusalem, in which occur the words, "Behold, your house is left unto you desolate." These correspondences afford good reason for the belief that our Lord's prophecies at Jerusalem were amplifications of the brief prediction spoken at Caesarea Philippi.

3. But there is yet another reason in support of the view stated above; and this reason I regard as conclusive. In foretelling those coming "days of vengeance," in which "all things that were written" were to "be fulfilled" (Luke 21:22), Christ gave His disciples a sign whereby they should know that the predicted days of vengeance were come, so that they might save themselves by flight; the sign being the encircling of Jerusalem with armies (v. 20). And then, in order to impress the lesson upon their minds, He spake a parable concerning the fig tree and all the trees, and said: "So likewise ye, when ye see these things come to pass, know ye that the Kingdom of God is nigh at hand. Verily I say unto you, This generation shall not pass till all be fulfilled" (vv. 31, 32). Thus we have Christ's own statement to the effect that the destruction of Jerusalem and the scattering of the nation was a coming of the Kingdom of God. And this He again coupled with the affirmation that his prediction would be fulfilled before the passing of that generation.

In studying the three accounts of our Lord's Olivet prophecy, the student should observe that the period designated in Luke's account "the days of vengeance," wherein there should be "great distress in the land, and wrath upon this people," is the same period that Mark designates "the days of affliction, such as was not from the beginning of the creation...unto this time" (Mark 13:19) and that is designated by Matthew the "great tribulation, such as was not since the beginning of the world to this time" (Mat. 24:21). The context of the several passages make it certain that one and the same period of unprecedented calamity is referred to in the three passages.

Comparison should be made also with Daniel's prophecy. "And there shall be a time of trouble, such as never was since there was a nation: and at that time thy people shall be delivered, every one that shall be found written in the book" (Dan. 12:1). The close similarity between the language of this prophecy and that of our Lord's Olivet prophecy gives assurance that both refer to the same event. The words of the angel to Daniel refer expressly to the Jewish nation ("the children of thy people"). Those who were to be delivered in that time of unparalleled distress-- those "found written in the book"--were, of course, the disciples of Christ, who took warning by their Lord's utterance, and fled for their lives when they saw His predicted sign. Happy for them they did not have some of our modern expounders of prophecy to instruct them as to the meaning of this prediction.

And particularly it should be observed, as fully confirming what is said above touching both the place, and also the time of that season of distress and tribulation, wherein all the prophecies of "wrath upon this people" were to be fulfilled, that the locality is expressly limited to JUDEA (Mat. 24:16), and that the time is expressly limited to THE GENERATION THEN LIVING (id. 34).

THE IMMENSE SIGNIFICANCE OF THE DESTRUCTION OF JERUSALEM

By pondering the Scriptures cited above the reader will be enabled to perceive the truly immense significance of the execution of God's long deferred, though oft threatened judgments and the pouring out of His wrath upon that nation which He had chosen for Himself, and with which He had dealt for a millennium and a half as He had never dealt with any other. For this was the nation He had so marvellously delivered out of Egypt; the nation to which He had given His holy law amidst the terrors of Sinai; the nation He had brought into the land of promise, driving out before them nations greater and mightier than they; to which He had sent His prophets with warning and with promises; and to which, last of all, He sent His only Son. And if one but calls to mind the many prophecies, beginning with Deuteronomy 28:49-68, that pointed to and were fulfilled in that stupendous event, (the destruction of Jerusalem) he will surely realize something of its unique place and importance in the scheme of God's dealings with mankind.

Finally, we have our Lord's own word for it that those were to be the days of vengeance wherein all things that were written should be fulfilled (Luke 21:22); and He was then speaking of a period that was to come within that generation; a period of great distress in the land (of Judea) and of great wrath upon that people. Hence the words "All things that are written" can mean nothing less than the many predictions of the prophets of Israel concerning the judgments that would be executed upon them if they persisted in their disobedience and apostasy.

To this also the Apostle Paul manifestly had reference when, writing to the Thessalonians, twenty-five to thirty years later, he said of the Jews that they "both killed the Lord Jesus, and their own prophets, and have persecuted us; and they please not God, and are contrary to all men", because of all which, "the wrath is come upon them to the uttermost" (1 Thess. 2:16).

THE DISCIPLES' TWO QUESTIONS

In view of all the foregoing, it seems clear that the first question asked by the disciples of their Master ("When shall these things be?") (Mat. 24:3) had reference to the demolition of the temple, whereof He had just spoken (v. 2); and that the other question ("And what the sign of Thy coming and of the end of the age?") had reference (a) to His "coming" for the destruction of the temple, and (b) to "the end of" the then elapsing Jewish age. For that coming judgment would be "the day of the Lord" for that people. It was an event such as the prophets of Israel might well have described in the very strongest

terms, and portrayed by means of the most impressive prophetic symbology.

THE TIMES OF THE GENTILES AND THEIR FULNESS

The destruction of Jerusalem marks not only the ending of the Jewish nation but also the beginning of "the times of the Gentiles." It is appropriate therefore to refer at this point to two expressions that are familiar to all students of prophecy: "The times of the Gentiles," and "The fulness of the Gentiles." The first occurs in a prophecy of Christ concerning the city of Jerusalem. The second is found in a prophecy of Paul concerning the Jewish people.

Our Lord, after having foretold the world-wide dispersion of the Jews, said:

"And Jerusalem shall be trodden down of the Gentiles until the times of the Gentiles be fulfilled" (Luke 21:24).

And Paul, after having set forth under the figure of an olive three the method of God's salvation for both Jews and Gentiles, said:

"I would not, brethren, that ye be ignorant of this mystery, let ye be wise in your own conceits, that blindness in part is happened to Israel, until the fulness of the Gentiles be come in" (Rom. 11:25).

The outstanding feature of each of these prophecies is that it describes a condition that was to last, in the plain sight of all mankind, throughout the entire era of the gospel. The first puts a conspicuous and age-long mark upon the city of Jerusalem. The other puts an equally conspicuous and permanent mark upon the scattered Jewish people.

My purpose is, in what follows, to show how, in the interest of dispensationalism, the significance of these exceedingly important Scriptures has been changed and the object for which they were given has been in a large measure frustrated. For these are prophecies of what was to be during this present age, and they are strictly limited thereto; whereas they are commonly treated as prophecies of what is to take place after this present age shall have come to an end. For our Lord's word concerning Jerusalem is generally interpreted as a prediction that, when the times of the Gentiles are ended, then Jerusalem will be repossessed by the Jews and will become the capital city of a revived Jewish nation. But in fact (and it ought not be necessary to point this out) the passage says not a word and gives not so much as a hint concerning what will happen to Jerusalem after the times of the Gentiles shall have come to an end.

Similarly the passage in Romans XI is often presented--not as a prophecy that was to be fulfilled throughout this gospel-dispensation, but--as a prediction that, after the work of the gospel shall have been completed, then the Jewish people are to be saved nationally and by a special salvation of earthly character, different from gospel-salvation. The passage, however, not only says not a word concerning a post-gospel salvation for the Jewish nation, but on the contrary teaches plainly that there is but one "common salvation" (Jude 3) for all men, viz, that figured by the olive tree of this passage.

A TWOFOLD WITNESS TO THE AUTHENTICITY OF BIBLE PROPHECY

Let it be noted that the fulfilment of these prophecies demanded the continued existence of both the city and the people, though sundered the one from the other, to the very end of the gospel era; and it demanded also that the city should be in the hands of strangers, and the people should be in the lands of strangers, during all that great stretch of time. Here then is a two-fold and a conclusive test of the Divine authorship of the prophetic Scriptures. For if, in the course of these "times of the Gentiles," either the city or the people had passed out of existence, or if the city had come into Jewish hands again or the Jewish people as a whole had changed their characteristic attitude towards Christ and His gospel, the prophecies would have been falsified and the entire New Testament discredited. On the other hand, seeing that none but God could have declared how it would fare with the city and people throughout this long age, these prophecies, by their fulfilment, furnish an unimpeachable witness to their Divine authorship, and hence to the Divine origin of the Book whereof they are an integral part.

A CONTINUING FULFILMENT

What gives these prophecies their surpassing value as witnesses to the Divine authorship of the Bible is the fact that they have the extraordinary character of demanding a continuing fulfilment. Prophecies which foretell the happening of a specific event--as the destruction of Jerusalem--are of no value at all as evidence until the predicted event occurs. And then the full effect is felt only by the generation living at the time. But these prophecies are of such a nature as to bear witness to every successive generation; and not only so, but are such that their testimony becomes more and more impressive as the centuries roll on.

Moreover, the fulfilment stands prominently before the eyes of the whole world. For Jerusalem is a conspicuous city; and so likewise as to the Jewish race, they are everywhere; and wherever they are, they are Jews, and known as such.

Therefore, God has made it possible by means of these two prophecies alone, even if there were no other proofs available, for all honest inquirers at all times throughout this gospel dispensation, to have convincing proof of the Divine inspiration of the Holy Scriptures; and particularly of the certainty of the predictive element therein.

"THIS IS JERUSALEM"

Special heed should be given to the fact that these prophecies relate wholly and exclusively to this present age. Our Lord, in the Olivet prophecy which we are considering as recorded in Luke's Gospel, foretold that there should be "wrath upon this people," that they should "fall by the edge of the sword," and "be led away captive into all nations"; and finally that Jerusalem should "be trodden down of the Gentiles, until the times of the Gentiles be fulfilled." And there His prediction ends. But in all the modern expositions I ever heard or read, the actual prediction of our Lord is virtually ignored, and He is made to say that when the times of the Gentiles are ended, then the Jews will be reconstituted as a nation, and will repossess their ancient homeland, with Jerusalem as their capital city. Thus a prophecy that is limited to a state of things which was to prevail during this present age, is converted into a prediction of a supposed state of things after the age shall have ended.

What our Lord took upon Himself to foretell in this prophecy is that the storm of judgment soon to break upon Jerusalem would not blot it out of existence, as Sodom and Gomorrah were obliterated, notwithstanding that her sin was likened to that of the cities of the plain (Isa. 1:10, and see Luke 10:12). Nor was it to be entirely abandoned and fall into ruins like Babylon and Tyre. Prophecy had previously declared concerning those famous cities (whose greatness and prosperity seemed to guarantee their permanence) that the former should become "heaps of rubbish," "a dwelling place for dragons," and be "no more inhabited forever" (Jer. 50:39; 51:37); and that the latter should be scraped bare and become like the top of a rock, and a place for the spreading of nets (Ezek. 26:4, 5, 21; 27:36; 28:19). And even so it was (and is) with those once mighty and flourishing cities. Jerusalem, on the contrary, though for its crimes it merited a severer punishment, was decreed to remain intact, but with a mark of Divine retribution abiding upon it (for it was to be perpetually in the hands of aliens), and thus was to serve as a conspicuous monument to the truth of God's word. Had the prophecies concerning the above named cities respectively been the products of mere human foresight, based upon the probabilities of the several cases, their terms would have been reversed, and the longer existence predicted of the Gentile cities.

As to what will befall Jerusalem after the times of the Gentiles are ended, I observe: (1) The Lord did not see fit to speak of that in this prophecy. This is a noteworthy fact; for had He meant to make known that the Jews were to regain possession of their ancient city, He would not have left the passage as it stands in the Bible. (2) Other Scriptures, moreover, reveal clearly that when the work of the gospel among the nations of the world is ended, the Lord will come again; that He will then remove His own redeemed people from this doomed earth, and will pour out the vials of exterminating wrath upon the rest. He Himself has pointed to the destruction of the earth in the days of Noah, and to that of Sodom in the days of Lot, as the typical foreshadowings of the universal judgment to come; and in so doing He laid emphasis upon the fact that the very day that Noah entered the ark "the flood came and destroyed them all," and "the same day that Lot went out of Sodom, it rained fire and brimstone from heaven and destroyed them all" (Luke 17:27, 29). It is certain therefore that when "the times of the Gentiles" are ended, there will be no Jewish people left on earth.

THE VAIL ON THEIR HEARTS

It was the Lord's decree from of old (Isa. 6:9-12; Mat. 13:14) that the people of Israel, because of their gross and long continued wickedness and rebellion, should be blinded and hardened to the Word of the Lord, The apostle Paul refers to their spiritually blinded state in figurative terms, saying that the veil which Moses put over his face now lies upon their hearts (2 Cor. 3:14, 15). And here (Rom. XI) he adds nothing to this but the fact that the predicted state of "blindness in part" was to continue "until the fulness of the Gentiles be come in" (v. 25). And there he leaves the subject. Again, however, as in the case already noted, modern expositors interpret the Scripture in such manner as to change its meaning in a material respect. For my experience has been that, when this passage is cited, it is not for the purpose of showing that the divinely imposed blindness of the natural Israel was to continue until the work of the gospel among the Gentiles should be completed; but for the purpose of lending support to the doctrine that there is to be a special salvation for the Jewish people (a salvation earthly in kind) after the day of gospel salvation is ended. But the apostle's next words (Rom. 11:26) are--not "and then all Israel shall be saved" (as it should read if this new teaching were true) but-- "And so all Israel shall be saved." To this deeply interesting passage we will return in a subsequent chapter.

Chapter Thirteen - He Limiteth a Certain Day

THIS brings us to a question of great interest, namely: When the times of the Gentiles are ended. What then? Will "the Day of the Lord" then come? Will Christ appear suddenly as a thief in the night, as the lightning that lighteneth from one part to another under heaven? Will the door of salvation then be shut? Will the dead be raised and righteous separated from the wicked? Will the eternal day of glory dawn, the New Jerusalem come from heaven, and the new heaven and new earth appear? Or is there to be, as is now commonly taught among evangelical christians, a post-gospel salvation for the Jewish nation, a salvation in which Gentiles also are to have a subordinate portion? For it is now taught that after this present era of the grace of God is ended; after the Gospel of Jesus Christ and the convicting and -regenerating power of the Spirit of God have done all they can do for the salvation of Jews and Gentiles (as between whom it is written that there is no difference"); then our Lord Jesus Christ will appear again in Person, and will be seen by the entire Jewish nation (for this doctrine puts the fulfilment of the prophecy, "His feet shall stand in that day on the Mount of Olives" into the next "dispensation") and the whole Jewish nation will be converted by the sight (Zech. 14:4). And after that wholesale conversion of the Jewish nation (which meanwhile is to be re-constituted in Palestine), those converted Jews are to go forth into all the world as missionaries to the Gentiles. (See the "Scofield Bible," note on Zech. 8:26).

By this same "authority" it is asserted that: "Israel as a nation always has its own place, and is yet to have its greatest exaltation as the earthly people of God" (note to Rom. 11:1).

And again: "According to the prophets, Israel, regathered from all nations, restored to her own land, and converted, is yet to have her greatest earthly exaltation and glory" (note to Rom. 11:26).

The order of these alleged future happenings, as given in this new "Bible" is: First, "The return of the Lord"; then "Restoration to the land"; and then "National Conversion" (note to Deut. 30:3).

And not only is there to be a salvation consisting of "earthly exaltation and glory" for the Jewish race, but the whole earth is to have a system of worship consisting of a revival of the sacrifices and other "shadows" of the law, which Christ (according to God's Bible) abolished by His sacrifice upon the cross (Heb. 10:1-9). For, according to the "Scofield Bible," Jerusalem is yet to be the religious center of the earth" (head line inserted above Zech. 8:20); and further it is asserted that:

"In the days when Jerusalem has been made the center of earth's worship, the Jew will then be the missionary, and to the very nations now called 'Christians'" (foot note on Zach. 8:23).

A RADICAL AND REVOLUTIONARY DOCTRINE

Here is modernism with a vengeance. Think of it, my brethren! For nineteen centuries it has been taught as one of the most indisputable of christian verities, that NOW is the day of salvation. But here is a copyrighted "Bible" that tells us of a coming day in which all the inhabitants of the earth will be saved and blessed; a day in which the most glorious triumphs of the Gospel of Christ will be made to look contemptibly cheap and insignificant; a day when conversion will be on a national, a wholesale, and a world-wide scale!

I protest against this doctrine, first of all because of its radical and revolutionary character; seeing that the teaching that there is to be another day of salvation, is subversive of foundation truth plainly taught in the New

Testament.

But besides this general objection, there are certain specific objections to be considered; among which are the following:

1. This new doctrine proclaims a salvation different in kind from (and of a distinctly inferior grade to) that "common salvation" ("common," that is, to all races and classes of men the world over) which the gospel of Jesus Christ offers to all men everywhere, upon the essential condition of individual repentance and faith.

2. The New Testament knows of but one salvation; and that salvation is identified with the gospel of Christ; which is expressly declared to be "the power of God unto salvation" (Rom. 1:16). And another scripture, speaking of Christ says, "Who hath abolished death and brought life and immortality to light through the gospel" (2 Tim. 1:10). And again, the apostle writes to the saints at Corinth concerning "the gospel...by which also ye are saved" (1 Cor. 15:1, 12). But, without further citation of texts, I give it as the indubitable teaching of the New Testament that "salvation" is of one sort only, without any "respect of persons"; and that it comes only "by the gospel" (Eph. 3:16). Hence, in setting forth a different salvation, apart from the gospel of Christ, this doctrine contradicts fundamental truth of the New Testament. Here then is a matter for the serious attention of all "Fundamentalists."

3. The doctrine in question proclaims "a second chance" for some who reject God's mercy now offered through the gospel. For whereas the New Testament, again and again, now in one form of words and now in another, declares that there is no salvation, no mercy, no hope, nothing but everlasting destruction from the presence of the Lord, nothing save the blackness of darkness forever, for those who reject the gospel, this doctrine says, not so, but that a whole generation of Jews who have not obeyed the gospel will be saved after the gospel day is over (to a lower grade salvation, to be sure, but such as the natural heart greatly prefers); and that Gentiles too will then be saved through the instrumentality of those Jews who are to be converted apart from the gospel; and not by faith, but by sight. In this respect dispensationalism resembles Russellism.

4. This doctrine sets forth a special salvation (earthly supremacy and dominion) for Jews only. Thus it builds again that "middle wall of partition" between Jews and Gentiles, thereby undoing the work of the cross of Christ, which broke that wall down (Eph. 2:14). In other words, it revives racial differences which God has abolished forever, and makes Him a "Respecter of persons" (2 Cor. 5:16; Mat. 12:50; Rom. 3:9, 22, 23; 10:12; Ac. 15:9; Eph. 2:14).

5. I have already indicated that the salvation thus said to be reserved for persons of Jewish descent, is more attractive to the natural heart than the salvation offered by the gospel. But it should be noted particularly that is the very thing the Jews had been taught by their blinded leaders to expect from their Messiah; and it was because He did not fulfil the prophecies according to their carnal misinterpretation of them, that they rejected and caused Him to be crucified. Hence this doctrine vindicates the attitude the Jews took towards Jesus Christ.

113

6. This new dispensationalism places the special salvation whereof it speaks in an era subsequent to that of the gospel; whereas the Scripture not only declares emphatically that "now is the day of salvation," which expressly limits salvation to this present era, but it also teaches impressively, and in various ways, that there will be no mercy for any when once the gospel day is ended. See Luke 13:23-2 7 (where the question was "are there few that be saved?"); Luke 17:26-30 (noting the words, "until the day," "the same day"); 2 Thes. 1:7-9, &c.

7. The new doctrine takes no account of the truth that Jews, like all other human beings, belong either to the first Adam, or to the last Adam; are either "in Adam" (where "all die") or "in Christ" (where "all are made alive"). Those Jews who are to be saved by this post-gospel salvation, are neither one thing nor the other. (This will be referred to more in detail hereafter). They are nondescript. Confessedly they have no part in the first resurrection, else they would be given glorified bodies, and be caught away to be with the Lord. Hence they must be "flesh and blood"; but if so, then they cannot have the Kingdom; for the same passage which describes the resurrection and transformation of those that are "in Christ," contains this emphatic declaration. "Now this I say, brethren, that flesh and blood cannot inherit the Kingdom of God; neither doth corruption inherit incorruption" (1 Cor. 15:50).

"NOW IS THE DAY OF SALVATION"

According to the teaching of the New Testament, salvation is strictly limited to this era of the Gospel. This has been briefly stated above; but it is of such importance as to call for further consideration. For the gospel-appeal derives its urgency from the revealed truth that there is but one day of salvation, and that it is now.. What else could be the meaning of those words of intensest earnestness: "Behold, now is the accepted time; behold, now is the day of salvation" (2 Cor. 6:2)? Could those words have been written if there were to be another "day of salvation" for any part of the human race? Certainly not.

And how could the apostle Peter have written that the Lord's seemingly long delay in fulfilling "the promise of His coming" was because He is "not willing that any should perish, but that all should come to repentance" (2 Pet. 3:9), if His coming was to be followed by day in which conversions are to be on a wholesale and national scale? if the modern doctrine of a Jewish millennium, whose blessings are to be shared by Gentiles, is the revealed truth of God, then the very reasons that are given to explain the great length of this present age (foreseen by Peter) would be compelling reasons why the Lord's coming should be hastened.

The apostle says that "the long-suffering of our God is salvation," which saying clearly places "salvation" on this side of the Lord's second coming. And then he appeals to the epistles of Paul as teaching the same thing (vv. 15, 16) ; adding the significant statement that there are in those epistles "some things hard to be understood, which they that are unlearned and unstable wrest, as they do also the other scriptures to their own destruction."

The Holy Spirit seems to have had this particular wresting of Paul's words that we are now discussing in view when He inspired the following Scripture:

"Again He limiteth a certain day, saying in David, Today, after so long a time, Today, if ye will hear His voice, harden not your hearts" (Heb. 4:7).

For here the Spirit of God uses the word "limiteth," which means to fix the boundary of something; and what God has fixed the bounds of in this case is "a certain day." Moreover, the context makes it plain that the "day" that God has specially marked off from other days is that wherein opportunity was to be given to men to enter into what He here calls "My rest," whereof David and other prophets had spoken. That "rest" yet "remaineth" (so the passage tells us) "to the people of God" (v. 9); and it makes plain that today is the time for entering into it (v. 11). That rest yet "remaineth" for the reason as here expressly stated, that "they to whom it was first preached entered not in because of unbelief"; and therefore men are now exhorted to "labour to enter into that rest, lest any man fall after the same example of unbelief."

That promised "rest" is what the Jews mistakenly supposed to be an era of earthly wealth and ease and world-leadership for themselves. And their error was fatal. How much more culpable then, the error of those who now adopt the same false interpretation of the prophecies, and who do it in the face of plain Scriptures like the one we are considering; which definitely limits the time for entering into God's rest to now; saying, "Today," and with the strong emphasis of repetition!

Beyond a doubt then, this passage teaches that there will be no entering into God's rest, that is, no salvation for any, after this gospel day shall have ended.

WHAT MANNER OF MEN ARE THESE?

In connection with this modern doctrine (modern among Christians, that is) of a future Jewish millennium, there arises an exceedingly perplexing question, namely: What sort of people are they who shall inhabit the earth during millennial times?

The "dispensational" doctrine is that the natural descendants of Jacob will be gathered back to Palestine, still in impenitence and unbelief (Zionism is supposed to be the beginning of this movement); that Christ will come to "the air" above (unseen), will raise dead believers, change the living and take all to glory (1 Th. 4:16, 17), thus leaving only unsaved persons on earth; that the "great tribulation" will then ensue and will last for seven years (this being the "missing week" of Daniel's seventy); that thereafter our Lord will continue His descent from heaven, will come visibly to the earth and take His stand on the Mount of Olives (which will thereupon be physically cleft into two parts, &c.) ; that the entire Jewish nation will see Him and be instantly converted after some fashion (see explanations below) ; that the Jews will then go forth and convert the nations of the earth; that all mankind will enjoy uninterrupted peace, plenty and every earthly gratification for a thousand years (all going to Jerusalem every year to keep the feast of tabernacles) during all which period of time the Jews will be in the place of leadership in the world. Out of this teaching (and I think I have fairly stated its main points as taught to me by men sound in the faith) there naturally arises the question already stated: What sort of people will these millennialites be? By the terms of the doctrine itself they will be just natural men, "Jews" and "Gentiles." They are not "in Christ"; for in Him there is neither Jew nor Greek. Therefore they must be "in Adam," and hence subject to death.

So far as I am aware the copious literature of those who propagate this doctrine of a Jewish millennium give no definite answer to the above question. I have, however, lately seen in print that the "tribulation saints" (those who go into the millennium, thus constituting a link between this "dispensation" and the next) are "a semi-Christian or semi-Jewish body, who will be called out as witness to God before the end of the present age." This is modernism truly; for the notion of a people who are half-Christian and half-Jew being called out as a witness to God, is a startling novelty.

Again, in a recent issue of an English periodical, which specializes in the doctrine of a Jewish national restoration during the millennium, there appeared an exposition of the words of Christ: "The hour cometh, and now is, when the true worshippers shall worship the Father in spirit and in truth" (John 4:23); concerning which verse the writer said:

"Observe, this statement leaves room for a change of dispensation back again to the locality of Jerusalem in millennial days."

So it does, indeed; and with equal truth it might have been said that the passage leaves room for a change of dispensation to the Sahara Desert.

And the writer proceeds to say that, in those "millennial days," the worship of God in spirit and in truth will be abolished the world over; and

116

the Levitical system--with its temple, altar, priesthood, feast days, and bloody animal sacrifices--will be restored at Jerusalem and will become the religion of all the nations on earth.

Thus the doctrine we are examining requires that, during those blissful millennial times, the light of the Gospel of Jesus Christ shall be wholly withdrawn from the earth. This is necessary because otherwise it would be impossible to interpret certain Old Testament prophecies literally, and make them fit into a post-gospel era.

But our expositor quoted above realized that it would not do to leave the matter there; so he hastens to inform his readers that, although the millenniumites will not be Christians, (he says it is "an error" to suppose they will be) yet the Jews of that day will be of a greatly improved type; that they will be: "no more rebellious or idolators. They shall be all religious; they shall be a nation of holiness, obeying the Lord's commands fully; kings and priests to the Gentiles...In all this is a great advance as it regards Israel." And how about the Gentiles?

"The same advance shall be found in regard to the Gentiles also. The remnant of the Gentiles shall own the superiority of Israel, and shall obey and worship the Savior. Idol-worship shall cease. Peace shall be enforced." (Is not this a contradiction of terms?) "They shall go up from year to year to worship at Jerusalem the Lord of hosts, and to keep the feast of tabernacles."

The Scriptures, however, know nothing of a third order of men, intermediate between the unregenerated children of Adam and the regenerated sons of God.

And what, we would ask, is the agency that will bring about this marvellous improvement in the dispositions and characters of men? What is it that will accomplish "what the law could not do?"

And finally let the reader notice the atrociously false doctrine that myriads of people--whole nations, both Jews and Gentiles--that have not obeyed the gospel of Christ, instead of being "punished with everlasting destruction from the presence of the Lord," are to be blessed with every carnal satisfaction and delight for a thousand years, including a religion suited to men in the flesh, being composed of forms and ceremonies and sacrifices, those "weak and beggarly elements," in which, even when they served temporarily a typical purpose, God declared He "had no pleasure" (Heb. 10:6).

But this topic of the resumption hereafter of the shadows of the law which Christ abolished by His Cross deserves a more extended consideration. Therefore I take up at this point the question:

117

ARE BLOODY SACRIFICES TO BE RESUMED HEREAFTER?

That the resumption of bloody sacrifices is a part of God's revealed plan for a future day is a prominent feature of the new "dispensational teaching"; and specifically it is taught that the sacrifices of bulls and goats, which Jesus Christ abolished by the offering of Himself as a Sacrifice for sin "once for all," are to be continued throughout the thousand years. It is ex plained that those animal sacrifices are to be carried on for a "memorial" of the Cross of Christ!

Thus in the "Scofield Bible" the following occurs in a note on Ezekiel 43:19:

"Doubtless these offerings will be memorial, looking back to the Cross; as offerings under the old covenant were anticipatory, looking forward to the Cross."

But what saith the Scripture?

"But now once in the end of the world hath He appeared to put away sin by the sacrifice of Himself" (Heb. 9: 26).

"For it is not possible that the blood of bulls and goats should take away sins. Wherefore, when He cometh into the world He saith, Sacrifice and offering Thou wouldest not, but a body hast Thou prepared Me. In burnt offering and offering for sin Thou hast had no pleasure. Then said I (in the volume of the book it is written of Me) lo I come to do Thy will, O God." And what was that will of God which He came to do? It is plainly stated in the word, "He taketh away the first that He may establish the second" (Heb. 10:4-9).

In the light of this Scripture it is plainly to be seen that the new dispensationalism contradicts the Word of God in respect to a matter of the first importance, namely, the consequences of the Sacrifice of Christ. For in the last quoted passages it is declared that the coming of Jesus and His offering of Himself as a sacrifice was for the very purpose of taking away those futile slaughterings of animals "which could never take away sins." Moreover, the wording of the verse last quoted above, indicates that the taking away of the shadowy and futile sacrifices of the Levitical system was necessary to the establishing of the Sacrifice of Himself as the true sin-offering. And finally, the teaching of the entire context (Heb. VIII-X) is to the effect that the Levitical system of sacrifices has been abolished forever by the one Sacrifice of Jesus Christ. Therefore the teaching of a future resumption of those sacrifices of bulls and goats, that have been abolished at such a cost, is serious error; and this is sufficient in itself to condemn the entire "dispensational" system whereof it is a part.

Chapter Fourteen - The Hope of Israel

BUT some will ask: How about all those promises to and concerning the people of Israel, especially the promises of the re-possession by them of the land God gave to their fathers?

The answer can be given in a few words:

(1) That most of those promises (if not all) were spoken before the return of the Jews from the Babylonian captivity, and many of them, including all such as were to have a literal accomplishment, were fulfilled in that event;

(2) That the promises concerning the possession of the land of Canaan were conditional upon faithfulness and obedience on the part of the people of Israel, who were repeatedly warned that if their hearts turned away from the Lord they should be plucked from off the land (Deut. 4:26; 8:19, 20; 30; 17, 18; Josh. 23:13; 16).

(3) Such of the promises of that sort as were unconditional are the heritage of the true Israel, the spiritual children of Abraham (Gal. 3:7, 29); and they have their fulfilment in the true land of promise, which the fathers of Israel had in view; for they were desiring--not the land of Canaan, or any other earthly territory, but--"a better country, that is an heavenly" (Heb. 11:16).

What then is the true "Hope of Israel?" To this question the Scriptures give as clear an answer as we could ask; and in order to find it we need not look beyond the passage where that expression is found, and the immediate context. For Paul, when taken as a prisoner to Come at the insistence of the leaders of the Jews at Jerusalem, called the chief of the Jews at Come together, and addressed them saying:

"For this cause therefore have I called for you, to see you and to speak with you; because that for THE HOPE OF ISRAEL I am bound with this chain" (Acts 28:20).

Was Paul then bound with chains and sent to Come for trial because he proclaimed and taught an earthly kingdom for the Jews? Turning back to chapter XXVI where he was answering for himself before Herod Agrippa, we find that, as Paul interpreted the Scriptures, the hope of the promise of God made to the fathers, "unto which promise all the twelve tribes" (true Israelites) "HOPE TO COME" was realized in the resurrection of Jesus Christ from the dead (Acts 26:6-8). And in proof thereof he related how he had seen the risen Christ outside the gates of Damascus, and had been charged by Him to preach the gospel to Jews and Gentiles, "to open their eyes, and to turn them from darkness to light, and from the power of Satan unto God." In brief, he preached as the hope or Israel the

Kingdom of God opened by the death and resurrection of Jesus Christ to believing and repentant sinners, both JEWS AND GENTILES.

And furthermore, when those leaders of the Jews there at Come desired to hear what his doctrine was ("what thou thinkest; for as concerning this sect, we know that everywhere it is spoken against"), a day was appointed, and

"there came many to him into his lodging; to whom he expounded and testified the kingdom of God, persuading them concerning Jesus, both out of the law of Moses and out of the prophets from morning till evening." (Acts 28: 21-23).

There is no uncertainty therefore regarding what Paul preached as the hope of ISRAEL.

Evidently then, the Jews of old and the dispensationalists of today were (and are) in error in giving to the Old Testament prophecies a literalistic interpretation.

For the language of the prophets is figurative and symbolical. In like manner when Jesus showed Nicodemus the true character of the Kingdom of God, asserting with the strongest emphasis that a man must needs be born again in order to enter it, He made use of terms which obviously were figures of speech taken from the familiar elements of nature, water and wind (i.e. breath, or spirit). His language, however, was utterly incomprehensible to that learned Rabbi, "the teacher of Israel," who accordingly manifested his astonishment thereat by exclaiming, "How can these things be?" (John 3:1-9); whereas, being the teacher of Israel, he should have known those things (v. 10).

It must be remembered that, to him, and according to the settled doctrine of all Jewish teachers of that day, the highest possible thing in the way of parentage was to be born "of the stock of Israel" (Phil. 3:3); and we must also remember that (to him) the essential condition for admission into the Kingdom of God was to be a natural descendant of Abraham, Isaac and Jacob. Hence he was quite unable to conceive how the prophecies and promises of God concerning that Kingdom could be fulfilled otherwise than by the national restoration of the Jews, and their exaltation to the place of dominance over the whole Gentile world.

So likewise today there are teachers who insist upon a naturalistic, or materialistic (they call it a literal) interpretation of the prophecies concerning the Kingdom, Israel, Jerusalem, etc. They too "cannot see" how this prophecy, or that, can be fulfilled except "literally"--that is, by regathering of the scattered Jewish people, their re-constitution into a nation as of old, and their re-investiture with the proprietorship of the land of Canaan. Thus they make their incapacity to see" the spiritual realities that correspond to the material types and figures used by the prophets, a rule for the interpretation of the prophecies.

It is not necessary, of course, to an understanding of the general voice of prophecy and of the general purport of the prophetic message, that one should know the meaning of every symbol and figure used by the prophets. All that is needed is that due heed be given to certain plain statements of the New Testament, and to the way the prophecies of the Old Testament are interpreted and applied therein.

For example, chapters VIII-X of Hebrews were evidently written in order to make known--and primarily to that saved "remnant" of Israel which had found deliverance through accepting Jesus as their Messiah-- that everything pertaining to the old covenant (people, land, city, sanctuary, priesthood, sacrifices, etc.) was but "a shadow of good things to come" (Heb. 10:1). This is quite enough to show that those who insist upon what they call a "literal" fulfilment of the promised blessings that were to come to "Israel" through Christ, have completely missed the mark. As says Joseph Butler (Butler's Analogy) commenting on Hebrews 8:4, 5:

"The priesthood of Christ, and the tabernacle shown to Moses in the mount, were the originals. Of the former of these, the Levitical priesthood was but a type; and of the latter, the tabernacle made by Moses was a copy."

And so with everything else: The new covenant has the eternal realities ("the originals") whereof the old covenant had but the temporary types or shadows. This being true (and the Epistle to the Hebrews makes the truth of it quite plain); and it being true also that Christ, by His death and resurrection has abolished that entire system of shadows, and has brought to light the spiritual and eternal realities typified thereby (Heb. 10:9), it follows that God's purposes are connected thenceforth with a regenerated people--"born of water and the Spirit"--a holy nation," who belong to a "heavenly country"; and with "a spiritual house," and a "Jerusalem which is above" (1 Pet. 1:3; 2:5, 6, 9; Heb. 12:22; Gal. 4:26, &c.). Abraham, Isaac and Jacob understood this (Heb. 11:9).

THE NATURAL AND THE SPIRITUAL

But it may be asked: Are there not prophecies which were to be fulfilled here on earth, and in connection with the earthly people of Israel, their land and their city? Such indeed there are; and hence arises the question: How can it be known with certainty whether a given prophecy relates to the heavenly "Israel" or the earthly? and whether its fulfilment is to be found in the spiritual realm or in the natural?

Most certainly there is need in many cases for the exercise of discernment, and for the seeking of light from the context and from other parts of Scripture. But the difficulty in such cases is not nearly so great as might be supposed. For, in the light of certain passages in the New Testament, it is clearly to be seen that the prophecies as a whole fall into two great divisions, whereof the first have their fulfilment in the sphere of the natural and the other in the sphere of the spiritual.

Thus it clearly appears from 1 Peter 1:9-12, that the prophecies in general had to do with these two distinct subjects, namely (1) "the sufferings of Christ," and (2) "the glories (plural) that should follow." And the passage also shows that the prophecies concerning "the sufferings" were to be first fulfilled, and then those concerning "the glories"; this being in agreement with the very explicit statement of 1 Corinthians 15:46, "Howbeit that was not first which is spiritual, but that which is natural; and afterward that which is spiritual."

Now it is evident upon reflection that the prophecies concerning Christ's "sufferings" must needs be fulfilled in the realm of the natural. For, as says the apostle, "Christ hath suffered for us in the flesh" (1 Pet. 4:1). Whereas His "glories" are in the realm of the spiritual and eternal. We have His own statement to this effect when, after His resurrection, He reproved two of His disciples for being foolish and slow of heart to believe all that the prophets have spoken. And He said:

"Ought not Christ to have suffered these things, and to enter into His glory? And beginning at Moses and all the prophets He expounded unto them in all the Scriptures the things concerning Himself" (Lu. 24:25-27).

Thus it is made clear that the death and resurrection of Jesus Christ and the coming of the Holy Spirit mark the dividing line where the fulfilment of prophecy, generally speaking (for there are some exceptions to which I will refer presently, which however do not affect the rule) passes from the natural into the spiritual realm.

Now it is specially to be observed that the era of our Lord's coming in the flesh was the time of the winding up of the affairs of the Jewish nation. That nation had its predicted part to perform in connection with "the sufferings of Christ." For it had been distinctly foretold that within the "determined" period of 490 years from the ending of the Babylonian captivity, "Messiah the Prince" should come, at which time they would "finish the transgression" (Dan. 9:24, 25). That this meant the completing of their national sin by the rejection and murder of their Messiah, is evident from Christ's own words, addressed to their leaders when they were plotting His death, "Fill ye up then the measure of your fathers"-- who had persecuted and slain the prophets--"that upon you may come all the righteous blood shed upon the earth" etc. (Mat. 23:31-36).

Then followed immediately His betrayal and crucifixion, and the rejection by them of the gospel preached with the Holy Spirit sent down from heaven. Their national sin culminated in the stoning of Stephen, which marked the termination of the "measured-off" period of seventy weeks of years. For the death of Christ took place, as foretold "in the midst of" the seventieth week (Dan. 9:27). From that time there remained, of all the prophecies relating to the natural Israel, only those foretelling the judgments of God that were to befall them, and specifically the destruction of Jerusalem and the temple, and their extermination as a nation, and the world-wide scattering of the survivors thereof. This was distinctly foretold by Moses (Deut. 28:49-64); and to the same effect is the prophecy of Christ, "And they shall fall by the edge of the sword, and be led away captive into all nations" (Luke 21:24). For the last word of prophecy concerning that people as a nation was fulfilled at the destruction of Jerusalem by the Roman armies.

There is a remarkable prophecy of this from the lips of Christ in Matthew 22:7 (a prophecy that is quite generally overlooked, though immensely important). There, in a prophetic parable, our Lord foretold how the Jews would treat those sent to them with the gospel, and then said:

'But when the King heard thereof, he was wroth: and he sent forth his armies and destroyed those murderers, and burned up their city."

That parable was spoken to the chief priests, Pharisees, and elders of the people (Mat. 21:23, 45; 22:1); and in the course of that same discourse Christ said to them plainly, "The Kingdom of God shall be taken from you and given to a nation bringing forth the fruits thereof" (21:43). That new "nation" came into being on the day of Pentecost; and it follows from all this (and from other scriptures that might be adduced) that all promises of blessing yet to be fulfilled belong to that "holy nation," that "peculiar people" (1 Pet. 2:9). For though there were yet a million promises of national blessing to be fulfilled, and though they all were in terms for the "Jews," every one of them would belong to the true "Israel of God."

From the foregoing it will be seen that there need be no difficulty in determining whether the fulfilment of a given prophecy is to be sought on the physical side of things (the "natural") or on the spiritual side; notwithstanding there may be much difficulty in construing the details of the prophecy.

SALVATION IN ZION FOR ISRAEL

It is easy, for example, upon the principles of interpreting prophecy stated above, to understand a prediction such as the following:

"1 will place salvation in Zion for Israel My glory."

This is the word of God through His prophet Isaiah (Isa. 46:13).

Three questions may properly be asked concerning this brief but vastly comprehensive promise:

(1)   What is this "salvation"?
(2)   Where is "Zion"?
(3)   Who are "Israel?"

WHAT IS SALVATION?

The word salvation is very comprehensive. It embraces far more than we are able to conceive of; for it includes all the blessings, joys and delights that God has prepared for His people, both here and hereafter. All the promises and purposes of God, whatsoever they be, are accomplished in and through Jesus Christ (2 Cor. 1:20) ; and it is most significant that the first reference in the New Testament to salvation is found in connection with the record of the Saviour's birth, and the Name He was to bear in His humanity: "Thou shalt call His name JESUS; for He shall save His people from their sins" (Mat. 1:21).

This (the forgiveness of sins) is therefore the first blessing of God's great Salvation. It has the place of prominence among the "better promises" of the New Covenant (Heb. 8:6, 10-12), whereof Jesus is "the Mediator"; and it was prominently in view at His birth.

It is also recorded that, before His birth, Zacharias, who was filled with the Holy Spirit, prophesied concerning Him, saying: "Blessed be the Lord God of Israel, for He hath visited and redeemed His people; and hath raised up an horn of salvation for us in the house of His servant David." And Zacharias goes on to declare that this was the fulfilment of what God had spoken by the mouth of His prophets from the very beginning, namely, "that we should be saved from our enemies, and from the hand of all that hate us (Luke 1:68-71).

This, be it noted, was a prophecy; for the record declares of Zacharias that, in so speaking, "he prophesied." (v. 67). That is to say, being "filled with the Holy Ghost" he spoke of God's salvation for His people as if the death and resurrection of Christ had already taken place, and as if redemption were already an accomplished fact. His words were: "God...hath visited and redeemed His people; and hath raised up an horn of salvation for us." For it is the customary manner of the prophets of God to speak of events yet in the future as having already taken place. For the prophets in their visions see events entirely detached from the sequence of other events to which they stand related in the course of time. It is exceedingly important to bear this in mind when studying prophecy.

To the same effect is Simeon's prophecy in the next chapter, who spoke to God of the infant Jesus as "Thy salvation, which Thou hast prepared before the face of all people; a light to lighten the Gentiles, and the glory of Thy people Israel" (Luke 2:28-32).

And to this agree the words of Paul, who, speaking in a Jewish synagogue (after the death and resurrection of Christ) referred to David and said: "Of this man's seed hath God, according to His promise, raised up into Israel a Saviour, JESUS" (Acts 13:22, 23). And further, on the same occasion he said: "And we declare unto you glad tidings (the gospel), how that the promise, which was made unto the fathers, God hath fulfilled the same unto us their children, in that he hath raised up Jesus again" (22, 32, 33).

The foregoing passages, and there are many like them, give an idea of what is meant in the prophetic scriptures by "salvation"; for they show that gospel salvation is what was intended. Further they make it clear that the time of the promised salvation for Israel is now, and not in some future era. And for further confirmation, I quote the words of Peter and the other apostles, spoken to the high priest and temple authorities at Jerusalem: "The God of our fathers raised up Jesus, whom ye slew and hanged on a tree. Him hath God exalted with his right hand to be a Prince and a Saviour, for to give repentance to Israel, and forgiveness of sins" (Acts 5:30, 31).

(II) WHERE IS "ZION"?

Isaiah also uttered a surpassingly beautiful prophecy concerning the days of Christ, which begins, "The wilderness and the solitary place shall be glad; and the desert shall rejoice and blossom as the rose" (Isa. 35:1), and which contains the express promise, "He will come and save you" (v. 4). Our Lord Himself fixed the time of the fulfilment of this particular prophecy by using its words in His message of assurance to His downcast forerunner (Mat. 11:1-1). In that passage the prophet foretells a "way of holiness," which was to be so plainly revealed that "the wayfaring men, though fools, should not err" in regard thereto; and in that connection says: "The redeemed shall walk there; and the ransomed of the Lord shall return (to Him), and come to Zion" (vv. 8-10).

The New Testament scriptures make clear in what sense the ransomed of the Lord return to Him and come to Zion." For the Holy Spirit speaks to those who look to Jesus as the Author and Finisher of their faith, and whom God owns as His children, saying: "For ye are not come unto the mount that might be touched, and that burned with fire"--Mount Sinai -- "But, ye are come unto Mount Sion...and unto Jesus" (Heb. 12:1-24).

For in short, Zion is where the Lord Jesus is; and God's salvation is there, because He is there; and therefore those who came to Him come to Zion. Thus we have the accomplishment of what David longed for when he said, "Oh that the salvation of Israel were come out of Zion" (Ps. 14:7, 53:6).

The apostle Peter likewise clearly locates for us the Zion of prophecy; for he says that those who come to Jesus Christ, raised from the dead, become living stones in that "spiritual house" which God is now building on Jesus Christ; and that this is the fulfilment of the prophecy of Isaiah which begins; "Behold, I lay in Sian a chief corner stone" etc. (1 Pet. 2:4-7, quoting Isa. 28:16).

Paul also makes it plain that the "Zion" whereof Isaiah prophesied is a heavenly locality. For he too quotes the words, "Behold, I lay in Zion," as being fulfilled in this present era (Rom. 9:33).

(III) WHO ARE "ISRAEL"?

In the light of the foregoing Scriptures it is plainly to be seen that the God of Jacob, in providing His great salvation at infinite cost, in placing it in Zion, and in calling "all Israel" (Acts 2:36) to come "to Mount Zion, and to the city of the living God, the heavenly Jerusalem" (Heb. 12:22), has grandly fulfilled, and in a manner and measure far beyond anything the mind of man could have conceived, all His gracious promises concerning Israel.

"But they have not all obeyed the gospel" (Rom. 10:16). They have not all responded to God's call to repentance and faith in Jesus Christ. True enough. And that is precisely what was foretold by Isaiah, whose words to that effect are quoted by Paul in Romans 9:27; namely, that only a small remnant of the natural descendants of Jacob would obtain the salvation of God. Hence the apostle says, "Israel hath not obtained that which he seeketh for; but the remnant hath btained it, and the rest were blinded" (Rom. 11:7). Here is a plain declaration that what had been promised to Israel had been obtained in Paul's day by the remnant, that is, the believing part of the people; whereas the mass of the nation had missed it because of the blindness of their hearts. Moreover, the context makes it clear beyond a doubt that what the apostle is speaking of is gospel salvation (10:1-3, 9-13). Therefore, what God had specially promised to Israel and what believing Jews (Paul among them) were receiving in those days was gospel salvation. But lest there should seem to be a discrepancy between the promise and the fulfilment, in that a small part only of the nation was being saved, Paul is at pains to explain that not all the natural descendants of Jacob were embraced in the "Israel" of prophecy; for that "they are not all Israel, which are of Israel"

(Rom. 9:6). As he had already declared in an earlier chapter: "He is not a Jew, which is one outwardly;...but he is a Jew, which is one inwardly" (2:28, 29). And furthermore, as stated in Chapter 4:11-16, the children of Abraham, as God reckons them, are those who have the faith of Abraham, whether by their natural birth they were Jews or Gentiles. And this truth is unfolded in detail in Galatians, Chapters 3 and 4; where, addressing Gentile believers, the apostle says: "And if ye be Christ's then are ye Abraham's seed, and heirs according to the promise" (Gal. 3:29)--that is, heirs of salvation in its comprehensive sense.

ISRAEL HATH NOT OBTAINED: THE ELECTION HATH OBTAINED

The verse cited above (Rom. 11:7) dispels all uncertainty as to how God fulfils His promises concerning Israel; so let us dwell a little further upon that verse:

What then? Israel hath not obtained that which he seeketh for; but the election hath obtained it, and the rest were blinded."

What Israel was seeking for was, of course, the fulfilment of God's wondrous promises of blessing and glory for His people; all of which had been summed up in the current phrase, "The Kingdom of God." Here then is the two-fold statement: (1) that Israel had not (up to that time) obtained the Kingdom, which statement, if it stood alone, would leave the possibility of their obtaining it in the future; and (2) that the election had obtained it, which leaves nothing of the unfulfilled promises of God for "Israel after the flesh." The "election," that is, as Paul carefully explains in the context, the believing "remnant" of Israel (the as many as received Him" of John 1:12) with believing Gentiles "grafted in," as represented by the "good olive tree" (v. 24), are the true Israel; and God had them in view all along as the inheritors of His Kingdom (1 Cor. 6:9, 10; 15:50; Eph. 5:5).

THE RIGHTEOUS NATION INHERITS THE PROMISES

The Jewish rabbis understood from Isaiah 26:2, and accordingly they taught, that the promises of God were for "the righteous nation which keepeth truth." But they took for granted that the natural Israel was that "righteous nation"; and it was of the essence of their doctrine that the Mosaic law had been given as the sufficient means for making Israel righteous. But the contrary truth, for which Paul mightily contended and which aroused their furious animosity against him, was that the righteousness that God demanded as the pre-requisite for inheriting His promises was--not the righteousness of the law, but--that of faith; even as it is written, "Abraham believed God, and IT was counted to him for righteousness" (Rom. 4:3).

And thus it was that "Israel, which followed after the law of righteousness, hath not attained unto the law of righteousness. Wherefore? Because they sought it not by faith" (Rom. 9:30-32). They missed everything; but in so doing they fulfilled the Word of God: "For they stumbled at that stumbling-stone; as it is written, Behold, I lay in Zion a stumbling-stone and rock of offence; and whosoever believeth in Him shall not be ashamed" (Rom. 9:33, quoting Isa. 28:16).

WHAT THEN? HATH GOD CAST AWAY HIS PEOPLE?

The apostle himself asks this question, and answers it. The answer is an emphatic NO. But does not this answer contradict the apostle's interpretation of the "allegory" of the two wives and two sons of Abraham; namely, that the bondwoman and her son should be "cast out," and that "the son of the bondwoman" (natural Israel) "shall not be heir with the son of the freewoman" (spiritual Israel)? Not at all.

The simple explanation is that God's "people," are those whom He foreknew, in other words, the believing remnant; and those He has not "cast away." The rest--the unbelieving mass--are not His people, and NEVER WERE. For though they were "of Israel" by natural descent, they were "not Israel"; which name properly belonged only to the spiritual seed of Abraham. "God hath not cast away His people which He foreknew"; and as to those "whom He did foreknow," Paul had already said (Rom. 8:28-30) that they are "those that love God, who are the called according to fits purpose."

From the foregoing it follows that, of all the as yet unfulfilled promises of God, whatsoever and how many soever they be, nothing remains for the natural Israel. All are for the true children of Abraham; even for them that are "of the faith of Abraham, who is the father of us all" (Rom. 4:16).

CONCERNING ZIONISM

In bringing to a close this chapter on the Hope of Israel it is appropriate to make a brief reference to the recent political movement known as Zionism, which has for its object the making of Palestine a homeland for the Jews. Concerning that movement a great deal of misinformation has been disseminated during the past twenty years in the interest of dispensationalism. For dispensationalist writers and speakers have painted wonderful word-pictures portraying the multitudes of Jews said to be flocking to their ancient homeland; the miraculously renewed fertility of the soil; the return of the early and latter rain etc. etc.; and it has been made to appear that the re-constitution of the Jewish State and the rebuilding of the Temple were matters of tomorrow or the day after.

All these supposed happenings were presented to eager readers and hearers as a marvellous fulfilment of prophecy taking place before our very eyes, and as giving assurance that the time of the end had come.

But the sober facts are that Zionism has been a pitiful failure almost from the beginning; and that in the period of its greatest success the volume of immigrants constituted but a trickling stream, and they were of the most undesirable sort. The movement reached its peak in 1926; and from that time to the present Zionism has been palpably a dying enterprise. A reliable magazine, Current History (April, 1927) gave from "a recent official report on trade conditions," an estimate of the population of Palestine for April 30, 1926; by which it appears that, after all the efforts of Zionism and the influence of the Balfour Declaration for ten years, and the help of other contributing causes (e.g. Russian persecutions) the total number of Jews in all Palestine was only 139,645; and they were outnumbered by Moslems more than three to one. The entire population was only 752,268; and the article states that "The country is under-populated and under-cultivated"; also that, "The season of 1925 was bad agriculturally owing to drought"; that various conditions "led to a shortage of capital and a depression which continued through 1926"; and that "the balance of trade was distinctly adverse."

Subsequent reports show that conditions have not improved; that the state of the Jews in Palestine is wretched in the extreme, and that the attitude of the great mass of Jews throughout the world towards the Zionistic project is that of complete apathy and indifference.

Chapter Fifteen - So All Israel Shall Be Saved

IN my comments on the words, "until the fulness of the Gentiles be come in" (Rom. 11:25) I pointed out that, notwithstanding that the passage in which those words occur is plainly a prophecy of the state in which the Jewish people were to exist throughout this present age, and that it says nothing whatever as to their state thereafter, it is now commonly interpreted as predicting that, in a future "dispensation," the whole nation is to be healed of its spiritual blindness. The next words of the passage are these:

"And so all Israel shall be saved: as it is written, there shall come our of Zion the Deliverer, and shall turn away ungodliness from Jacob; for this is My covenant unto them when I shall take away their sins.

As concerning the gospel, they are enemies for your sakes; but as touching the election they are beloved for the fathers' sakes." (Rom. 11:26-28).

This passage likewise has been very badly treated in the interest of the new dispensationalism. And, like as the preceding passage has been transmuted from a prophecy strictly limited to this age into one relating wholly to a future age, so this passage also is lifted bodily out of the age where the Spirit of God has placed it, and is transported to a future age, an age which exists only in the imagination of men. For the passage is usually interpreted precisely as if it read, "And then all Israel shall be saved," instead of "And so all Israel shall be saved."

Indeed all that is needed for the correction of this gigantic "dispensational" error is first to note the significance of that little word "so," and then to ascertain its meaning from the context, which is easily done.

The adverb "so" answers to the question "How?" It says nothing at all in answer to the question "When?" Yet my experience has been that, whenever Romans 11:26 is cited by dispensationalists, it is presented as proof that the entire Jewish race, reconstituted into an earthly nation, is to be saved in a future "dispensation." In fact, however, the passage teaches the very opposite; namely: that the phrase "all Israel" means, not the entire Jewish race of a future age, but the entire body of the redeemed of this gospel age. The word "so" occurs in the concluding part of the passage and hence necessarily refers back to the preceding verses, where the apostle, after explaining who they are that constitute God's true "Israel," tells in detail, and illustrates by the figure of the "good olive tree," just how God's Israel was to "be saved." He there describes beforehand precisely what God has been doing from that day to this; and when he finished his description, and has illustrated it with marvellous clearness by the figure of the olive tree, he brings the matter to a conclusion by saying: "And so"--that is, in the manner he had been describing--"all Israel shall be saved." And he adds that the saving of "all Israel" in that manner would fulfil certain Old Testament prophecies, which he quotes.

If therefore we simply ascertain from the preceding verses (as can be done with little trouble and with certainty) who are the "all Israel" of God's purpose, and how they were to "be saved," we shall also ascertain in the process when they were to be saved.

WHO ARE THE "ALL ISRAEL" OF ROM. 11:26?

The "all Israel" of Rom. 11:26 is the whole body of God's redeemed people. It is composed of "the election" (which, as we have seen, has "obtained" what the natural Israel as a whole had "not obtained") with the addition thereto of believers from among the Gentiles. For the main purpose of this passage (Rom. IX-XI) and that also of chapter IV, and likewise of Galatians (chapters III and IV) is to make known that the real "Israel," the true "children of Abraham," who inherit the promises of God, are not the natural seed of Abraham but his spiritual seed.

Paul proves his doctrine, and at the same time exhibits the great difference between Abraham's natural seed and his spiritual, by citing the historical fact that "Abraham had TWO sons" (Gal. 4:22); and from the Old Testament records of the very different things that befell Ishmael and Isaac respectively, Paul deduces the great difference, in the purposes of God, between the unbelieving mass of the Israelitish people (answering to the son of the bondwoman) and the believing "remnant" (answering to the son of the free-woman). For those things, the apostle tells us, "are an allegory," the meaning of which he proceeds to explain (Gal. 4:21-31).

Abraham's elder son, Ishmael, represents the natural Israel, those "born after the flesh." Ishmael had the first-born's place in Abraham's house for a number of years before Isaac, who was to be the true and sole heir, was born. And during all that time, which answers to the period from Sinai to Pentecost--that is the era of the old covenant--Ishmael was the heir apparent of all that Abraham had. Moreover, even after Isaac appeared upon the scene, Ishmael continued for a time in occupation of the premises, and took advantage of his position to persecute the true heir. The period when Ishmael and Isaac were both under one roof and the former still had the status of a son and heir of Abraham, answers to the time from Pentecost to the destruction of Jerusalem. For during that period the natural Israel, "the son of the bondwoman," still occupied the holy land and city, and "persecuted" the true Israel (Gal. 4:29; 1 Thess. 2:15).

But that era of the overlapping of "the two covenants" was of short duration. For "what saith the Scripture? Cast out the bond woman and her son: for the son of the bond woman shall not be heir with the son of the free woman" (Gal. 4:30). And the next verse gives us the application of the incident: "So then, brethren, we are not the children of the bond woman, but of the free."

The meaning of the words, "shall not be heir," is free from all uncertainty. Those words mean that the promises of God to Abraham are all for his spiritual seed. And this, moreover, is precisely what the apostle had already said in plain language: "Know ye therefore that they which are of faith, the same are the children of Abraham" (3:7). "And if ye be Christ's, then are ye Abraham's seed, and heirs according to the promise" (3:29). The same truth is plainly taught in Romans 4:13-16.

Coming now to Romans IX-XI, it is the plain teaching of that passage (1) that God's true "Israel," the nation concerning which it is said, "And so all Israel shall be saved," is the whole body of the redeemed of the Lord: and

(2) that, that body is composed of the believing "remnant" of the natural Israel (the "remnant according to the election of grace," Ch. 11:5) with the addition thereto of believing Gentiles. Those two elements, so diverse and antagonistic by nature, are incorporated into a spiritual unity, "the unity of the Spirit" (Eph. 2:12-18, 4:3). And this is according to that "mystery" of God's eternal purpose, which was not clearly revealed in ages past, but now is made fully known (Eph. 3:4-6). That "mystery" is what is graphically illustrated by the olive tree of Romans XI. And as regards the salvation of the natural Israel in a future era, so far from teaching that doctrine, the passage we are studying was written for the purpose of refuting it. This will very clearly appear in what follows.

This section of the Epistle begins with the declaration of a fact which caused the apostle great heaviness and continual sorrow in his heart, namely, that "they are not all Israel which are of Israel" (9:6). Observe here the phrase, "all Israel," concerning which we are now inquiring. And observe further that what we here are told is, not what it includes, but what it does not include. The "all Israel" of this passage does not embrace all who are Israelites. Paul is here speaking of his "kinsmen according to the flesh, who are Israelites" (ver. 3, 4). And what caused him such acute anguish of mind was the fact, revealed to him by the Spirit of God, that not all these, but indeed only a few of them, were to be included in the "all Israel" of God's purposes. It is simply impossible that Paul could have penned those words of poignant grief; it is impossible, I say, that he could have wished himself "accursed from Christ" for the sake of his "kinsmen according to the flesh" if he had held and was about to declare the doctrine now frequently attributed to him, namely, that all the Israelites in the world were to be saved at the second coming of Christ--an event the christians of that day regarded as imminent. That doctrine, which was the very corner stone of the Judaism of that day, Paul had cast aside; and it was moreover an important part of his ministry to expose the falsity of it.

The next two verses (Rom. 9, 7, 8) make the matter still clearer. There we read: "Neither because they are the seed of Abraham are they all children: but 'in Isaac shall thy seed be called.' That is, they which are the children of the flesh, these are no; the children of God: but the children of the promise are counted for the seed."

This calls for no explanation; for it is the Spirit's own explanation. We need only to observe that the reason why the truth here stated caused the apostle such acute distress was that it so rigidly excludes from God's salvation all the natural descendants of Abraham except the few who were of the faith of Abraham (Rom. 4:13-16) that is, those who believed the gospel.

The apostle then proceeds to make known that it had been God's plan and purpose from the beginning to save--not all the natural descendants of Abraham, but--only such as He should choose. And here we have the doctrine of "election" (Rom. 9:10-26) which takes its name from the fact that God makes an "election" or choice, from among Jews and Gentiles, of those He will save and have eternally as His own people. This principle of God's sovereign choice is illustrated by the case of Esau and Jacob (vv. 10-13) where His choice was made before the children were born.

In the closing verses of chapter IX (27-33) Paul returns to the matter that was causing him such acute sorrow, namely that, as Isaiah had prophesied, "Though the number of the children of Israel be as the sand of the sea, a remnant (only) shall be saved." That remnant is the Jewish part of "the election"; and thus we have a clear light upon verse 26 of Chapter XI; for the words "a remnant shall be saved," explain the words, "all Israel shall be saved."

In chapter X the apostle, after expressing the desire of his heart and his prayer to God for Israel "that they might be saved," goes on to show that none can "be saved" except by believing the gospel ("the word of faith which we preach," v. 8); and that in respect to this vital matter there is "no difference between the Jew and the Greek. For whosoever shall call on the Name of the Lord shall be saved." And the chapter closes with a strong intimation that the Israelitish nation as a whole would not be saved; the word of Jehovah to that nation being, "All day long I have stretched forth My hands unto a disobedient and gainsaying people" (v. 21).

Special heed should be given to the first part of chapter XI. It shows that God's rejection of Israel nationally does not warrant the conclusion that God has cast away His people. For, as we have already seen, God's part of the nation, that is, the election, He did not then cast away, and never will. Hence, in bestowing upon "the election" what had been promised to "Israel," God was fulfilling His promises strictly in accordance with their true intent. The result is that "Israel hath not obtained that which he seeketh for; but the election hath obtained it, and the rest were blinded" (11:7).

Seeing therefore that "the election," by believing the gospel of Christ, has obtained (and certainly will never be deprived of) that which God had promised to "Israel," it is clear that "the remnant according to the election of grace," with believers from among the Gentiles added, is the "Israel" of the prophetic Scriptures. Indeed it is evident, upon an impartial study of the entire passage, that its main purpose is to make known that very fact.

And this purpose stands forth in the clearest light in the figure of the olive tree, whereby the apostle, at the end of the passage, illustrates the truth he has been expounding. That olive tree represents "the Israel of God," "the election," the "one body" of the redeemed. Not all who are of Israel are in it. On the contrary, many of the natural branches, "because of unbelief were broken off" (v. 20). And on the other hand, many believing Gentiles are included; these being the branches of "the olive tree which is wild by nature, which branches have been "grafted contrary to nature into a good olive tree." This is the fulfilment of all God's purposes and promises, the final outcome of all His dealings in grace with both Jews and Gentiles.

And now, in seeking an answer to the question, Who are the all Israel that are to be saved? We have found also the answer to the other question. Flow shall they be save? For, as we have seen, the passage teaches in the plainest way that they are to be saved by believing in Jesus Christ. And in so teaching, it simply affirms the foundation truth of the Gospel, namely, that there is no other way of salvation; for "he that believeth on the Son hath everlasting life; and he that believeth not the Son shall not see life; but the wrath of God abideth on him" (John 3:36). The natural branches of the olive tree were broken off "because of unbelief," and any of them that are saved, must be saved by personal and individual faith; for there is no other way.

Furthermore, in saying that "God is able to graft them in again," and that He will do so "if they abide not still in unbelief" (v. 23), the passage bears a clear witness to the truth that there is no other salvation for them but that which the olive tree represents. This verse alone forbids the idea that there is, or can be, a national salvation for the Jewish race in some future era. God, in His great forbearance and long suffering (II Pet. 3:9, 15) still keeps open to them the door of salvation, so that individual Israelites, by personal faith in Jesus Christ, may enter in and be saved. But when He rises up and shuts that door, then they who begin to seek Him for salvation will hear Him say, "1 know you not; depart from Me, all ye workers of iniquity," and it was to Jews He said this (Luke 13:25, 27).

Furthermore the word "So," in Romans 11:26, meaning in the manner described above and illustrated by the figure of the olive tree, plainly answers the question, How all Israel is to be saved. They will "all be saved" precisely "SO," and not otherwise.

And finally we have found also, in what has been set forth above, the answer to the question, "When shall they be saved?" For, seeing that all Israel shall be saved so--that is, by means of "the word of faith" which the apostles preached, then most certainly they must be saved ere this day of gospel-salvation comes to an end. And this is plainly declared in other Scriptures, as has been shown above.

Chapter Sixteen - Translated Into The Kingdom of the Son

IT has long been my conviction that the present day weakness of God's people, their internal disorders and divisions, and the utter failure of their collective testimony to the world, are mainly due to the fact that they are not instructed and established in the great truth declared in the opening verses of Colossians, namely, that when God received those who believed "the word of the truth of the gospel" (v. 5), He delivered them "from the power of darkness" (a kingdom) and translated them "into the Kingdom of His dear Son" (v. 13).

This is fundamental gospel-truth; and it behooves all "Fundamentalists" to take due note thereof.

It is truth that gives glory to the exalted Son of God, "the King, eternal, immortal, invisible" (1 Tim. 1:14). It is truth that assures the people themselves as to their perfect security. It is truth that was intended to carry conviction to all men that Jesus Christ is truly the One sent of God (John 17:21). Therefore nothing is more urgently needed at the present hour than that this basic truth, now so generally neglected, should have given to it, in the ministry of Christ's servants, something like the prominence given to it in the New Testament Scriptures.

THE KINGDOM NOT THE CHURCH THE BASIS OF UNITY

What is commonly emphasized by orthodox teachers at the present time is that those who are saved through faith in Jesus Christ are forthwith incorporated into the Church; which is the body of Christ, and is also the spiritual temple now being built "for an habitation of God through the Spirit" (Eph. 1:22, 23; and 2:22). This is truth indeed, and truth of superlative value. But it belongs not in such close association with the gospel as the subject we are considering. For the Scriptures connect the Gospel directly with the Kingdom rather than with the Church. The message that conspicuously marked the beginning of this era which is specially characterized by the forgiveness of sins (the era of the New Covenant) was "the Word of the Kingdom" (Mat. 13:19), John the Baptist had prepared the way by his "baptism of repentance for the remission of sins" (Luke. 3:3). And Jesus was anointed King and was sent to Israel "to preach the gospel to the poor;" and Himself said, when the people besought Him not to depart from them: "I must preach the Kingdom of God to other cities also; for therefore am I sent" (Luke 4:18, 43).

Furthermore the preaching of the Kingdom of God was the chief business of the apostles and evangelists, as may be seen by consulting the record given us of the ministry of Paul (Ac. 13:22, 23, 32-34; 17:7; 19:8; 20:25; 28:23, 41; Rom. 14-17; I Cor 4:20; 15:50 Col. 1:12, 13; 2 Tim. 2:8 &c. &c.). Indeed that apostle expressly says that the gospel is preached for "the obedience of faith" (Rom. 1:5, marg. and 16:26); and further, that the particular object of his own ministry was "to make the Gentiles obedient" (15:18). Those who believed the gospel were said to have become "obedient to the faith" (Ac. 6:7), to have "obeyed from the heart" (Rom. 6:17). And on the other hand they who are doomed to "everlasting destruction away from the presence of the Lord," are they who "obey not the gospel" (2 Th. 1:7-9). The word obedience expresses a kingdom-relation. It is the state of heart of those who confess Jesus Christ as Lord, which none can do "but by the Holy Ghost" (1 Cor. 12:3).

Now it is most needful for us to observe that, whereas the Kingdom-- that is, the relation of the redeemed of the Lord to God's Anointed King-- was the prominent theme of the preaching and teaching of the Lord Himself and of His apostles, the subject of the Church (that is, in the comprehensive and eternal sense of that word, not in the local sense) was not developed until the latter part of Paul's life; until in fact his active ministry was ended. For it was during his imprisonment in Come that he wrote the Epistle to the Ephesians, in which that great truth is unfolded. Prior to that we have on the subject of the Church (in this all-inclusive sense) only the brief and unexplained statement of Christ, "On this rock I will build My Church; and the gates of hell shall not prevail against it" (Mat. 16:18).

The main conclusion properly to be drawn from the facts briefly set forth above is that the subject of the Kingdom of God is of the very essence of the gospel of Christ, and is of immediate and vital importance to all mankind, both to them that are within and to them that are without; whereas the subject of the Church (as God's spiritual house now being builded) is of interest only to those who have been already translated into the Kingdom; and for them it has not the same direct and practical bearing upon their life down here as has the truth pertaining to the Kingdom. For the Church (in this broad sense, for we are not speaking at all of the local churches) belongs rather to eternity than to time (Eph. 5:27; Rev. 21:23); for it is as yet unfinished, being now in process of formation. Whereas the Kingdom belongs to the present; for Christ is reigning now. Hence, if this immensely practical truth were given its rightful place in the preaching and teaching of Christ's ministers, it would tend to unify the divided people of God.

SALVATION A CHANGE OF ALLEGIANCE

By Colossians 1:12, 13 we are given to know that a complete change takes place in a man's allegiance, that is, in his governmental or political relations with the invisible "principalities and powers" (v. 16), when he believes on Jesus Christ through "the word of the truth of the gospel, which" (says the apostle) is come unto you, as it is in all the world" (vv. 5, 6). It is "the Father" Himself Who makes that change of relationship; and the change includes two acts of sovereign and almighty power: first, He delivers, or sets free from the "power"--that is to say, from the rule or dominion--"of darkness" (to which all men are by nature in subjection); and second, He translates those He has thus set free from their natural allegiance into the Kingdom of His dear Son--that is to say, He transports them as it were bodily across the otherwise impassable frontiers of the domain of sin and death, and places them safely and securely in "the Kingdom of His dear Son."

Is it possible to exaggerate when speaking of the stupendous change that God has brought about in the kingdom relationship, or allegiance of one who has received Jesus Christ as His Saviour and Lord? Impossible. And on the other hand, can truth so vital, so practical, so fundamental, be slighted without bringing weakness, division, suffering and loss to the people of God, and ruin to their collective testimony? Assuredly not. And it were well we should call to mind in this connection, that loyal devotion to the person of a sovereign, and love of the country of one's birth, are sentiments which, when opportunity for expressing them is given, make even timid souls as bold as lions, and impel them to deeds and sacrifices of the loftiest heroism. But where, it will be asked, are the heroes of faith in our day? My answer is, that the material is here even as it was in the days of the apostles, and that what is lacking is that gospel which was preached by them "with the Holy Ghost sent down from heaven" --the Gospel of the Kingdom.

"PRESENT TRUTH" (2 Pet. 1:12).

This, I say, is truth of immediate and practical importance; and for the reason that, not only is it closely connected with our personal salvation, but it has to do with the honor of our Saviour, Lord and King, Jesus Christ, Who is "the Author of eternal salvation unto all them that obey Him" (Heb. 5:9).

The Scripture makes it plain that the grand object of Christ's redemption is the recovery of man from out of that state of disobedience into which the whole race fell through Adam's transgression ("by one man's disobedience," Rom. 5:19), and his restoration to a state of obedience. That state of disobedience and alienation from God is spoken of in the Scriptures as a kingdom, or "dominion"--"the dominion of sin and death," "the power of darkness," "the power of Satan" --; and the state of obedience or subjection to God, into which those who believe the gospel are brought by the door of the new birth (John 3:5; I Pet. 1:23), is also a kingdom--the Kingdom of God.

The basis of man's "reconciliation" to God (for by nature we are all His "enemies") was laid in "the death of His Son" (Rom. 5:10); and by "the gospel of God concerning His Son," the blessed truth of reconciliation is proclaimed to the whole world (2 Cor. 5:18-21) ; and all men are bidden to return to obedience, or in other words to enter the Kingdom of God. It is thus we are saved; for salvation means to be under the protection of God's King.

THE OBEDIENCE OF FAITH

Reference has been made above to Scriptures which declare that the gospel is preached for "the obedience of faith"; and now it remains only to point out that the obedience of faith is a very different thing from legal obedience. The main difference is that the particular kind of obedience which the gospel demands (and which it also elicits) is free and voluntary, the spontaneous obedience of the heart. THIS HEART OBEDIENCE IS THE VERY ESSENCE OF SAVING FAITH. In fact, saving faith and heart obedience are one and the same thing. For to "obey" and to "believe" are hut various renderings in English of the very same Greek word. So likewise, "unbelief" and "disobedience" are different renderings of the same word in the original text. Obedience "from the heart" (Rom. 6:17) is what distinguishes faith from mere orthodoxy that is, from the mere holding of correct opinions and the giving of a mere intellectual assent to the statements of God's Word. For true faith is not a creed, or a matter of opinion, however correct and orthodox, but a thing of heart and life and deeds; manifesting itself in "works of faith," that is, acts of spontaneous obedience to the Word of God. Thus it is written that "by faith Noah being warned of God...prepared an ark to the saving of his house"; that "by faith...Abraham obeyed"; "by faith Moses kept the passover and the sprinkling of the blood"; "by faith" the children of Israel "passed through the Red Sea as by dry land" (Heb. 11:7, 8, 28, 29). By these instances, and by many others, God has plainly shown that true faith is a live, active, energetic thing; its most distinctive characteristic being that it acts spontaneously--without coercion or the constraint of pains and penalties for disobedience--in strict accordance with the Word of God; rendering prompt and unquestioning obedience to His commands, even when they run counter to human wisdom and to the desires of the natural heart. "Of such is the Kingdom of heaven."

Brethren, it is "this gospel, of THE KINGDOM" that is to be "preached in all the world for a witness unto all nations; and then shall the end come" (Mat. 24:14). Can the preaching of any other gospel accomplish the purposes of God? Impossible. Nay, we can, and we must, put it even more forcibly; for we read of some who had been "moved from him that had called them into the grace of Christ unto another gospel, which is not another." (Gal. 1:6, 7). For any other gospel than that which calls men "into the grace of Christ" is not a "gospel" at all. And the gospel that calls men into the grace of Christ is that which calls them into the Kingdom of God's dear Son. For testifying "the gospel of the grace of God," and "preaching the Kingdom of God" are the same identical thing (Acts 20:24, 25).

THE END

www.ingramcontent.com/pod-product-compliance
Lightning Source LLC
LaVergne TN
LVHW011356080426
835511LV00005B/316